D0613636

The Flavor of WISCONSIN

FOR KIDS

TERESE ALLEN AND BOBBIE MALONE

Wisconsin Historical Society Press

Published by the Wisconsin Historical Society Press
Publishers since 1855

© 2012 by the State Historical Society of Wisconsin

Publication of this book was made possible in part by a grant from
the Amy Louise Hunter fellowship fund.

For permission to reuse material from *The Flavor of Wisconsin for Kids*, 978-0-87020-493-7, please access
www.copyright.com or contact the Copyright Clearance Center, Inc. (CCC), 222 Rosewood Drive,
Danvers, MA 01923, 978-750-8400. CCC is a not-for-profit organization that provides licenses and
registration for a variety of users.

wisconsin**history**.org

This book is intended for children's use under the supervision and guidance of a responsible adult.
Although the authors have included standard safety guidelines as part of the recipes, neither the
Wisconsin Historical Society nor the Wisconsin Historical Society Press is liable for any injuries, losses,
or other damage resulting from using the information in this book.

Photographs identified with WHi or WHS are from the Society's collections; address requests to
reproduce these photos to the Visual Materials Archivist at the Wisconsin Historical Society,
816 State Street, Madison, WI 53706. A list of other illustration credits can be found on pages 184–185,
which constitute a continuation of this copyright page.

Back cover: WHi Image ID 17137

Printed in the United States of America
Designed by Shawn Biner, Biner Design
Cover illustrations by Michael Custode

16 15 14 13 12   1 2 3 4 5

Library of Congress Cataloging-in-Publication Data
Allen, Terese.
  The flavor of Wisconsin for kids / Terese Allen and Bobbie Malone.
       p. cm.
  Adapted from: The flavor of Wisconsin / Harva Hachten and Terese Allen. 2009.
  Includes index.
  ISBN 978-0-87020-493-7 (hardcover : alk. paper) 1. Cooking, American. 2. Cooking—Wisconsin.
3. Children—Nutrition. 4. Wisconsin—Social life and customs. I. Malone, Bobbie, 1944– II. Hachten,
Harva. Flavor of Wisconsin. III. Title.
  TX715.A44275 2012
  641.59775—dc23
                                       2011033625

∞ The paper used in this publication meets the minimum requirements of the American National
Standard for Information Sciences—Permanence of Paper for Printed Library Materials,
ANSI Z39.48–1992.

To my nephew and kitchen pal Jack,
a.k.a. Snack Pack, Jack Pot, and My Butter

—Terese

For Bill, my sweetheart and partner
in discovering the many flavors of Wisconsin

—Bobbie

Contents

Before You Start

A backyard tea party for two in Chippewa Falls, around 1900

Kindergartners at Dudgeon School in Madison made yummy pumpkin pie in 1945.

1. The recipes in *The Flavor of Wisconsin for Kids* are designed for children and adults to prepare together. Make sure that an adult is present during all the steps of each recipe.

2. Although all the recipes in this book are things that kids will enjoy making as well as eating, some are easier to do than others. To know if a recipe is very easy or a bit more challenging, look for the key at the beginning of each recipe: means that the recipe is very quick and easy to do, means that it takes a little longer and involves a little more skill, and means that you'll be using a number of different kitchen skills to make the dish and should expect to spend more time working on it. And an means that you need heat, usually from an oven or stovetop, to prepare the recipe. A recipe with a does not require heat and is suitable for use in a classroom or other group activity setting.

3. Read all the way through each recipe once or twice before you begin working on it. Do you understand all the instructions? If not, ask the adult who is working with you to explain them to you.

4. Make sure that your work surface, such as a kitchen counter or table, is clean and uncluttered.

5. If you have long hair, tie it back out of the way.

6. Wash your hands with soap and water before handling any food. Dry them on a clean towel. If you handle raw meat or eggs as part of your recipe preparation, wash and dry your hands again before you touch anything else.

7. Wash and dry any fruits and vegetables you will be using in your recipe.

8. Gather everything you'll need to make the dish you've chosen. Measure out all the ingredients and put them in bowls or on dishes until it's time to add them. Place all the tools and equipment you'll need nearby, too, including oven mitts or pot holders to handle hot pots and pans, and trivets or wooden boards that you can put hot dishes on when you take them out of the oven.

9. Be especially careful when using sharp knives. Use the right size knife for the job (an adult can help you determine this), and make sure the knife is sharp enough to cut whatever it is that needs cutting. Use cutting boards to protect your work surface—one cutting board for raw meat and a different one for fruits and vegetables. Hold the food you're cutting steadily and securely, with your fingers safely away from the blade. Always cut with the sharp edge of the blade moving away from you. When you're done with your slicing or chopping, clean the knife immediately and put it away.

10. When cooking on a stovetop, turn pot and pan handles so they don't hang over the front edge of the stove. If you mistakenly bump into a sticking-out handle, the hot ingredients in the pan can spill out, making a big mess and possibly burning you. (Plus, you'll have to start the recipe over.)

11. In many recipes, you can add salt and pepper "to taste." That means you should sample the food before you serve it, and decide whether you think it would taste better if it was a little more salty or peppery. If you add these seasonings, do so only a little at a time, then taste again and decide if you should add a little more. But don't sample anything containing meat or eggs that aren't completely cooked yet—the bacteria in raw animal products can make you sick. And if you want to take a taste of something hot, make sure you let it cool down before putting it in your mouth. Nothing tastes good with a burnt tongue!

12. Clean up as you go along: wipe up spills right away, and wash your tools and equipment as soon as you're finished using them. This way, you'll have practically finished cleaning up by the time you're ready to eat. Spending less time cleaning up at the end will let you start enjoying your delicious kitchen creations sooner!

In Wisconsin, cheese is a work of art!

Have you ever made butter, like these second graders were doing in 1950? See the recipe on page 106!

What does Wisconsin taste like? The flavor of the state comes from its land and its people. These two main ingredients—land and people—are the sources of many familiar and not-so-familiar foods that you will learn about in this book.

Did you know that foods have their own stories, shaped by where each food comes from? These stories help us remember that the foods we eat come from our waters, soils, and forests. They also come from the people who have hunted, gathered, and cultivated foods here, or who brought food traditions with them when they moved here from other places.

In this book you'll find out how to cook many different kinds of Wisconsin foods. And when you eat them, you'll not only taste delicious dishes, you'll also get a real taste of Wisconsin history, geography, and culture.

Look carefully at the cover of this book. You can find a mini food story within each letter of WISCONSIN. The basket of apples inside the **W** hints at the many orchards that supply us with lots of varieties of apples each fall. The fish in the **I** could have been swimming in one of the Great Lakes on our borders or one of the many waterways within our state. The **S** contains a picture of a young woman holding a wheel of cheese made from the milk produced on our dairy farms. These dairy farms started in the late 1800s when immigrants from Europe and New York arrived here with their milking and cheese-making skills. We have them to thank for making us into cheeseheads!

The next two letters, **C** and **O**, tell stories of hunting and gathering. Both the deer and the wild rice tell us that Native people

Warm summer days and crisp autumn nights make Wisconsin a wonderful place for growing apples!

depended on our natural resources long before non-Indian people began moving to and settling in Wisconsin. These foods remain important today to both Native and non-Native people. The **N** shows people enjoying egg rolls at a festival. Hmong people and other folks who have moved here more recently have added terrific new tastes to our Wisconsin food heritage. In the **S**, you can see the maple tree being tapped for its syrup. Both Native and non-Natives have long appreciated the wholesome sweetness found in our forests. The final letters, **I** and **N**, contain scenes familiar to us all: food from Wisconsin farms and gardens. Gathering and gardening are two ancient practices in our region that have grown popular once again today, as part of the "eat local" movement.

Surrounding the letters in WISCONSIN, you can see part of a cherry pie (made from delicious Door County cherries) and an ear of yummy corn on the cob (grown on farms all over our state). Both are reminders of how important agriculture is in Wisconsin.

Like the many foods on the cover, this book is a feast of Wisconsin stories. Each chapter describes the places and the people who make up the flavor of Wisconsin. As you read, cook, and eat from this book, you'll learn about Wisconsin's land and people, both past and present. You may even discover more about your own roots in our state— about your family's food traditions, and how and why your family settled here. After all, you're part of the flavor of Wisconsin, too.

We invite you to dig in and enjoy the feast!

What does Wisconsin taste like to you?

CHAPTER 1

Flavors from Forests

FOR A BRIEF TIME in the late 1800s and early 1900s, Wisconsin was one of the centers of the world's timber industry. This means that Wisconsin's forest lands provided much of the world's wood for building construction and other uses. Forests of pines dotted with smaller stands of spruce and hemlock covered most of the northern part of Wisconsin. Farther south were hardwoods—large-leafed trees that lose their leaves in fall—such as birch, maple, and oak.

Forests have supplied food as well as building materials in Wisconsin for thousands of years. Animals that lived in the woods were hunted for food. The woods were full of all kinds of berries: sumac, bunchberry, blueberry, chokeberry, sand cherry, blackberry, raspberry, strawberry, and Juneberry. Each spring, wild mushrooms and edible wild greens would begin to poke up from the forest floor, and maple trees flowed with sweet sap. During their seasons, hazelnuts, black walnuts, beechnuts, butternuts, and hickory nuts covered the ground.

Fall birch trees show their colorful leaves.

Hunting

Early Indians in Wisconsin, and others who followed, hunted for survival. Native hunters knew that many kinds of animals also feasted on forest foods, so they found it easy to spot deer, rabbits, squirrels, black bears, beavers, raccoons, foxes, wolves, skunks, quail, and wild turkey, for example. Indians throughout Wisconsin history brought home whatever they could to supply their families with meat.

Here's a joke from Indian country. Question: "Do you know what they call vegetarians in Indian country?" Answer: "Bad hunters!"

Thousands of years before non-Indians came to the area, Indians here hunted with spears. About two thousand years ago, Indian groups began hunting with bows and arrows instead of spears. Some Indian and many non-Indian hunters today still enjoy bow hunting.

Early Wisconsin Indians carved and used these spear points to hunt.

The Indians used every part of the animals they killed: meat for food, bones for tools, and hides for clothing or to meet other household needs. To dry meat, Indians cut it into thin strips. Then they wound these strips around sticks. Finally, they hung these sticks over—but not too close to—an open fire. Drying meat kept it preserved in the years before refrigeration.

Archaic Indians were the earliest deer hunters.

When immigrant and non-Native settlers moved to Wisconsin, they too became active hunters. Game hunting of all kinds remains extremely popular. Today, both Native and non-Native hunters in central and northern Wisconsin hunt black bear, probably the biggest wild game. Other than wild turkey—hunted in both spring and fall—most hunting takes place in fall and winter. Small game includes grouse and pheasant in the north central area and squirrel and rabbit everywhere in the state. You'll read about waterfowl (birds that live near water) in chapter 2.

Deer hunting, especially, has remained a tradition in many Wisconsin families in part because it's an activity that grandparents, parents, and children can share. Children listen to stories of past hunts and learn hunting techniques and safety procedures from the adults, and families get to enjoy outdoor recreation together.

Today, small meat markets and butcher shops around the state process venison (deer meat) for hunters. They make some into summer sausage, brats, and other tasty foods. Because people today are concerned with healthy eating, low-fat venison is in more demand than in past decades. Without deer hunting, some of these small meat markets would not be able to compete with larger supermarkets for customers.

Rabbit hunters show off their catch in the early 1900s.

Many Wisconsin kids begin hunting at an early age.

Successful hunters proudly pose by their cabin in the late 1800s.

Foraging for Food

Foraging is searching for and gathering food that grows wild. Foraging can be fun, but it can also be dangerous. It's fun to find food: wild onions or wild asparagus in the spring, raspberries or blackberries in the summer, and nuts in the fall, for example. But foods like mushrooms have poisonous varieties as well as delicious ones, so it's best to avoid them all and leave that foraging to experts.

Spring is the time of year to find the first edible shoots, such as ramps. Ramps have large, long leaves at one end, a reddish stem, and a white bulb that looks like the root end of a green onion. In fact, since ramps are one of the first greens to show up in spring, they are quite welcome when found at a local farmers' market. Ramps are a variety of wild leek, and they taste garlicky—delicious with scrambled eggs or sautéed in butter and served with just about anything. Other early spring wild greens include wild sorrel, nettles, and dandelion greens. Nettles can sting you when they are fresh, but not after they have been cooked.

All of these tasty wild greens help you get over the winter indoors-too-much blahs!

One of the best things about the long, lazy days of summer is finding plenty of berries—so good that they often don't make it into the bucket or basket you might be carrying to hold them. Do you think the Indians living here thousands of years ago were better

Ramps from a local farmers' market make a delicious spring treat.

Summer's the perfect time to pick raspberries.

More than a hundred years ago, Ojibwe families made extra money picking blueberries.

In Search of Morels

A variety of mushroom known as the morel is probably the most desired of all foraged food in Wisconsin, both because morels are delicious and because they are rare. What makes them rare? First of all, morels have a very short season in the damp days of May. Second, morels grow all over the state, but they grow most successfully in southwestern Wisconsin. That's because it's the Driftless Area. The last glacier didn't reach and reshape the Driftless Area's many hills and deep, damp valleys. That geography plus Wisconsin's typical weather are ideal for mushroom growth. Muscoda, on the banks of the Wisconsin River, claims to be the state's morel capital. Third, morels blend in with their environment so that even when you're in their neighborhood, you have to search very carefully to spot them.

People looking for morels often wait until "oak leaves are the size of squirrels' ears." When spring temperatures and sunlight have made oak leaves grow to this size, conditions are also good for morels to grow. Experienced foragers look on sun-warmed, south-facing slopes of hills, among the branches of dead elm trees, in old and neglected apple orchards, or even in open fields. The morel has a very distinct cone-like and wrinkled cap that makes it difficult to mistake once one is spotted.

When mushroom hunters get their morels back home, they soak them in cold water to get rid of dirt and bugs, dry them gently on paper towels, and then fry them in a little butter. If you ever get a taste of morels cooked in butter, you'll understand just why all that foraging is worth the effort!

But remember—never hunt for or eat wild morels unless you have an adult with you. Morels are not poisonous, but many other kinds of mushrooms are. You must be very sure that you have the real thing.

The rare morel mushroom is hard to find during its very short season.

at keeping more of these small delicious fruits for winter? They dried berries of all kinds to use for seasoning and sweetening during the rest of the year. Today we can keep these summer treats in the freezer to enjoy in winter.

When leaves begin to fall and you see squirrels burying acorns, remember that Indians in the southern part of the state washed acorns, roasted them, and chopped them to use in soups or ground them to make a kind of flour. Few people eat acorns these days, but many gather hickory nuts, black walnuts, and butternuts. All of these are delicious additions to hot cereals or baked goods.

Maple Sugaring

The Ojibwe, Menominee, and other Wisconsin Indians looked forward to winter's end when sap began to rise in maple trees. A traditional Great Lakes Indian Wenebojo story talks about how Native people began tapping maple trees.

As the story goes, Nokomis was the grandmother of Wenebojo. She taught him how to insert a small piece of wood into maple trees so the sap could run down to be caught beneath. Wenebojo tasted the thick syrup and found it deliciously sweet. He told his grandmother that this was too easy, and that Indians should have to work to get this wonderful syrup.

An artist created this illustration of an Indian sugar camp of many years ago.

Wenebojo climbed to the top of one of the maples, then scattered rain over all the trees to dissolve the sugar as it flowed into the birchbark vessels. Now the Indians had to cut wood, make vessels, collect the sap, and boil it for a long time. If they wanted the maple syrup, they had to work hard for it.

When the sap was rising, Indian families packed up their supplies of dried meat and their birchbark buckets, sap spikes, and other equipment to move to sugar camps. These camps were in the "sugar bush," an area with many maple trees. That's where Indians went to tap maple trees and make syrup and sugar. To tap a tree, someone had to cut a small horizontal gash in the tree trunk about three or four feet above the ground. Then a cedar spike was pounded in at an angle to allow the sap to flow into a birchbark container, known as a mocock, placed under it.

Stones were heated on fires, then placed into the sap containers to heat the sap. As the rocks cooled down, the people kept replacing them with hot ones. Finally, when the sap turned into a thick syrup, it was done.

When French and French-Canadians began coming to Wisconsin in the late 1600s, they came because of the fur pelts Indians were willing to trade for European goods like woolen blankets and cooking pots. During this period of the fur trade, Native people often replaced their birchbark containers with European-made metal kettles that could be placed on fires and kept boiling day and night.

The thick syrup that resulted from either method had to be strained, then boiled again to get even thicker. Some of the syrup was also poured into birchbark cones or molds to harden into cakes. Some of it was made into granules that were more like today's sugar. While the syrup was still warm, it was carefully poured into birchbark containers. It had to be stirred and stirred with a big wooden paddle until it changed into granules. Indians made and used more maple sugar granules than maple syrup.

Indians used mococks such as this one when they made maple sugar.

Native people used maple sugar for much more than simple treats. They used it as a seasoning for fruits, vegetables, cereals, fish, and meat. Indians didn't have salt until fur traders brought it with them to Wisconsin. In the summer, Native people dissolved maple sugar in cold water and mixed it with the sap from other trees to make a refreshing summer drink.

Elizabeth Fisher Baird was born in Prairie du Chien in 1810. Her father was a fur trader, and her mother was part Odawa Indian. Elizabeth grew up speaking three languages: French, English, and Odawa. As an older woman, she wrote down her memories of growing up. She shared one of these memories of going to her Odawa grandmother's sugar camp on Bois Blanc Island, about five miles east of Mackinac Island in Lake Huron. Elizabeth remembered that the camp was "in the midst of a forest of maple, or a maple grove. One thousand or more trees claimed our care, and three men and two women were employed to do the work."

Elizabeth described in great detail the entire process of making sugar. She said that pouring the syrup into the birchbark containers, or mococks, was "especially difficult; only a little could be made at a time, and it was always done under my grandmother's immediate supervision."

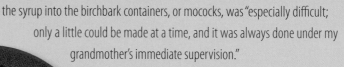

While most maple sap collected today is turned into syrup, very little was kept for that purpose when Elizabeth was growing up. She said that it was boiled very thick to keep it from souring. "For summer use it was put in jugs and buried in the ground two or three feet deep where it would keep a year, more or less." Aren't we lucky to be able to keep our Wisconsin-produced maple syrup in our refrigerators!

Elizabeth Fisher lived in two cultures, Indian and non-Indian.

Although the equipment for tapping maple trees has changed, the running of the sap has not. Maple sap flows best when the weather brings sunny days with temperatures in the 30s and 40s and nights in the teens and 20s. Warmer days and colder nights make the trees swell and contract, pumping out liquid in the heartbeat rhythm of the maple forest. The season is over as soon as the maple trees begin to form buds. But you can enjoy maple syrup on your pancakes or in your oatmeal long after the maple trees bloom—thank goodness!

It's fun tasting sap tapped from a maple tree.

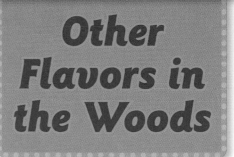

Other Flavors in the Woods

In the early days of the timber industry in the late 1800s and early 1900s, lumberjacks worked in Wisconsin's Northwoods. Their job was cutting down the huge pine forests—and later the hardwoods—for the valuable trees that would supply lumber to build the growing towns and cities of the Midwest. Lumberjacks lived in logging camps set up right in the woods where they worked. They slept in a bunkhouse and ate their meals in a large dining hall. The cook and his helper, the cookee, had to make large meals to give the lumberjacks plenty of food to fuel their hard work. Breakfast was probably the most important meal of the day.

John Nelligan worked in logging camps most of his life. He remembered breakfast as "no such light meal" as fruit and cereal. Instead, a crew of hungry lumberjacks needed mountains of pancakes, beans, fried potatoes, coffee, and biscuits. "Lumberjacks were always well fed," John later wrote. "The better they were fed, the better the work they did." You can imagine how good that food must have tasted before the men went out to work, and how they welcomed the warm dinners filling their stomachs after a hard day in the woods.

Lumberjacks needed lots of good food to keep them going all day in the woods.

Italian-Style Venison Meatloaf

8–12 servings

When immigrants move to a new land, they miss the foods of their own country. So they prepare dishes from their homeland that are familiar and comforting to them. Hmong egg rolls and Mexican tamales are two examples of traditional dishes made by immigrant families in their new homes.

Sometimes immigrants cook American dishes but they change them to make them "taste like home." For instance, this recipe for an American favorite, meatloaf, has Italian flavors in it (such as garlic and Parmesan cheese). Think of it as an Italian immigrant's recipe for an American food.

Notice that this meatloaf is made with venison (deer meat). Some immigrants hunt for wild game in their new land, just as they did in their old country. It's part of their tradition. Eating wild game reminds them of home.

In Wisconsin, hunters look forward to the gun deer hunting season, which runs for a little over a week in November.

Ingredients:

1 egg

2 pounds ground venison or ground beef
   (or use 1 pound of each)

1 cup dried breadcrumbs

½ cup finely chopped onion

½ cup grated Parmesan cheese

2 teaspoons minced garlic

1 teaspoon salt

¼ teaspoon black pepper

1 cup Italian tomato spaghetti (marinara)
   sauce, divided

You Will Need:

Knife

Large baking pan with sides

Large bowl

Measuring cups and spoons

Whisk or fork

Directions:

1. Heat oven to 350 degrees. Oil a large baking pan (one that has sides).

2. Crack the egg into a large bowl and beat it with a fork or whisk.

3. Add the ground meat, breadcrumbs, onion, Parmesan cheese, garlic, salt, and pepper and stir gently. Stir in ½ cup of the spaghetti sauce. Mix lightly until everything is well mixed. (You can use your hands, but wash and dry them first!)

4. Turn the meat mixture out onto the baking pan. Use your hands to shape the meat into a flat-topped loaf or thick rectangle. Spread the remaining ½ cup spaghetti sauce over the top of the meatloaf.

5. Bake 50–55 minutes. To test for doneness, insert a knife in the thickest part of the meatloaf and peek inside. There should be no pink meat showing. Let the meatloaf stand 5 minutes before serving. If there's fat at the bottom of the pan, spoon or pour it off before serving.

Venison Chili

10–12 servings

A drive along
a country road in
Wisconsin, especially around
sunset, is a good time to spot deer.

Does anyone in your family go hunting for deer? Or do you have a friend or neighbor who does? Deer hunting is a yearly custom for many families in Wisconsin. When a deer is shot, the hunter typically brings the animal to a butcher shop. There the deer is skinned and the meat is ground or cut up and frozen. Sometimes the meat, which is called venison, is made into summer sausage, which is good with cheese and crackers. A deer provides a lot of meat for a family to eat.

Chili is a popular dish that can be made with venison. This recipe makes a venison chili that is thick and rich, like a stew. It tastes best when you make it the day before you're going to eat it. Try serving it over macaroni. It's delicious!

Directions:

1. Heat the pot over medium-high heat for 2–3 minutes. Add 1–2 teaspoons of oil to the pot and tip the pot so that the oil spreads across the whole bottom.

2. Add about one-quarter of the ground meat. Brown the meat, breaking it up into small bits with a spoon or metal spatula as it cooks. When it's done, remove the browned meat from the pot and place it in a bowl.

Ingredients:

2–3 tablespoons vegetable oil, divided

3 pounds ground venison or lean ground beef

2 cups chopped onions

1 jalapeño pepper, seeded and finely chopped (optional)

1 tablespoon minced garlic

1 can (15 ounces) kidney beans, drained

1 can (15 ounces) pinto beans, drained

1 can (1 pound) refried beans

6 cups bottled vegetable cocktail juice

2 teaspoons ground cumin

2 teaspoons chili powder

$\frac{1}{8}$ – $\frac{1}{4}$ teaspoon cayenne pepper (optional)

Salt and black pepper (optional)

You Will Need:

Large, heavy soup pot or Dutch oven

Measuring cups and spoons

Plastic gloves

Wooden spoon

Metal spatula

Large bowl

3. Cook the rest of the meat in batches as described in step 2. When you've browned all the meat and taken it out of the pot, pour about 1 tablespoon oil into the pot and reduce the heat to medium. Add the onions, jalapeños, and garlic and cook them, stirring often, until they are wilted and tender. This will take 5–10 minutes.

4. Transfer the browned meat back into the pot (leave behind any fat that has collected in the bowl). Stir in all the beans, vegetable cocktail juice, cumin, and chili powder. If you want some extra spiciness in the chili, add a little cayenne pepper, also.

5. Bring chili to a simmer. Cover it partially with a lid. Let it simmer slowly for 1–2 hours. Stir it occasionally as it simmers. If it gets too thick, add some water.

6. When the chili is done, taste it and add some salt and black pepper if you think it needs it.

Caution

Be sure to use plastic gloves when you are working with jalapeños.

Rabbit (or Chicken) with Mushroom Sauce

6–8 servings

This is the kind of dish that frontier families might have made. One family member might have hunted the rabbit while another gathered the wild mushrooms in the woods. They could harvest the vegetables and herbs from their garden and get the cream from the family cow. They even could churn the butter from some of the cream.

Today, most people would purchase the ingredients for this dish from a grocery store. They might buy the rabbit at a farmers' market or a butcher shop (or use chicken instead of rabbit, since today fewer people eat rabbit than in times past). But wherever you get the ingredients for this dish, it is a special preparation. Serve it with boiled noodles or mashed potatoes.

Directions:

1. Heat 1 tablespoon of the butter or oil in a large, heavy skillet over medium-low heat. Add the onions and cook until tender.

2. Raise heat to high, add the mushrooms to the pan, and sprinkle them with salt and pepper. Cook the mushrooms, stirring often. Liquid will come out of them as they cook. Keep cooking them until they are tender and most of the liquid is gone.

3. Place the cooked onions and mushrooms in a bowl. Let the skillet cool slightly, then wipe it out with a towel or paper towel.

Ingredients:

3 tablespoons butter or oil, divided

½ cup chopped onion

½ pound button mushrooms, rinsed clean and sliced (about 3 cups total)

Sprinkling of salt and pepper

2 cups flour

1 tablespoon salt

½ teaspoon black pepper

1 rabbit (or you can substitute chicken), cut into 6–8 pieces

⅔ cup chicken stock

¼ cup heavy cream

1 teaspoon chopped fresh sage or ½ teaspoon dried sage

You Will Need:

Measuring cups and spoons

Knife

Large, heavy skillet with lid

Wooden spoons

Medium bowl

Towel or paper towels

Paper bag

Tongs for turning meat

4. Place the flour in a paper bag. Add 1 tablespoon salt and ½ teaspoon pepper. Shake the bag to mix up the flour and seasonings. Place rabbit or chicken pieces in the bag. Shake the bag to cover the pieces with flour.

5. Heat the remaining 2 tablespoons butter or oil in the skillet over medium-high heat. When the butter or oil is hot, add the floured rabbit or chicken pieces. Brown them 4–6 minutes on the first side. Turn and brown them on the other side, 4–6 minutes longer.

6. Stir chicken stock into the pan. Cover and simmer, turning the meat occasionally, until done. This will take 15–20 minutes. To check for doneness, poke the meat near the center with a fork. The juices that run out should be clear. If you see any pink, cook the meat longer.

7. When the meat is done, add the onions and mushrooms, cream, and sage to the pan. Simmer for several minutes until everything is hot.

Barley with Mushrooms

10 servings

Ingredients:

5 tablespoons butter, divided

¾ pound fresh button mushrooms, rinsed clean and sliced (4–5 cups total)

1 teaspoon salt

¼ teaspoon black pepper

6 cups stock or broth (chicken, beef, mushroom, or vegetable), divided

½ cup chopped onions

1 cup pearl barley

You Will Need:

Colander
Paper towels
Knife
Cutting board
Large skillet
Wooden spoon
Large and medium saucepans, with lids

Mushrooms grow in the woods in many parts of Wisconsin. Polish and Russian families who moved here in the 19th century were glad to find mushrooms growing in the area, because they loved mushrooms. Indeed, they were very skilled at finding wild mushrooms. They knew the edible ones from the poisonous ones. They often dried their mushrooms and stored them for the winter. Here's a dish many Poles liked to make; they called it *kuba*. This recipe calls for button mushrooms, which are sold in grocery stores (not gathered in the wild).

Directions:

1. Melt 2 tablespoons butter in a large skillet over medium-high heat. Add the mushrooms and cook them, stirring often, until they are tender. Stir in the salt and pepper and set the mushrooms aside.

2. Prepare the barley: First, heat the stock in a medium saucepan and keep it hot on a back burner of the stove.

3. Heat the remaining 3 tablespoons butter in a large pot over medium heat. Add the onions and cook them until tender, stirring often, about 10 minutes.

4. Stir in the barley and half of the hot stock. With the pot lid off, simmer the mixture until most of the liquid is gone, stirring occasionally.

5. Add the cooked mushrooms and remaining stock. Simmer the barley, stirring it once in a while, until the liquid is absorbed and the barley is tender. This will take 30–40 minutes. If the barley begins to dry out before it's done, add a little water. If the barley is tender before all the liquid is gone, raise the heat to boil off the liquid.

Creamy Scrambled Eggs with Ramps or Green Onions

8 servings

Ramps are wild leeks. They have long, wide green leaves, a red stem, and a white onion-like bulb at the end. They grow in clumps in Wisconsin woodlands during springtime. Ramps taste something like garlic, but they're not as strong-tasting as regular garlic. If you take a walk in the woods in May and smell garlic in the air, look down! You might be walking on ramps.

Directions:

1. Crack the eggs into a large mixing bowl. Add the half-and-half, salt, and pepper. Use a whisk to mix until smooth.

2. Melt butter in a large nonstick skillet over medium-low heat.

3. Add the chopped ramps or green onions to the pan. Cook them, stirring often, until they look wilted.

4. Reduce the heat to low. Pour the egg mixture into the pan. Cook the eggs slowly, stirring often, until eggs are set—that means that no liquid egg is showing and the egg mixture looks dry (but not dried out). This should take 15–20 minutes. Cooking the eggs slowly will make them extra creamy.

Ingredients:

12 large eggs

¼ cup half-and-half

1 teaspoon salt

¼ teaspoon black pepper

4 tablespoons butter or
¼ cup olive oil

2 ramps or 3 green onions,
finely chopped

You Will Need:

Large mixing bowl
Whisk
Large nonstick skillet
Knife
Cutting board
Wooden spoon

Wild Berries and Honey

Any number of servings

John H. Fonda was a trader who traveled the Wisconsin wilderness from 1820 to 1840. One day as he was hiking in the woods, he came upon a tree filled with honeycombs. It was a happy day for him! He melted the honey in his campfire kettle and used it as a sauce for prairie hens that his traveling partner had cooked. Fonda wrote about the meal: "I have always been blessed with a good appetite, but on that occasion it must have been a little bit better than usual, for after eating my bird . . . [and a] fair ration of dried meat and parched corn, I thought it better to fill the kettle again with honey, by way of dessert. That evening I got honey enough for a life time." Imagine eating all that honey!

What do you eat with honey? Have you ever tried it with wild blueberries or strawberries? Like John Fonda's honeycombs, wild berries can be found in the woods. Wouldn't it be fun to find a patch?

Summer on Madeline Island meant fun gathering raspberries at Grant's Point.

Ingredients:

Blueberries, strawberries, blackberries, or
   other fruit (wild or bought)

Honey

Fresh mint leaves (optional)

You Will Need:

Colander
Small serving bowls
Spoon for drizzling
Knife
Cutting board

Directions:

1. Rinse the berries and let them drain in a colander.

2. Divide the berries into small serving bowls.

3. Drizzle a little honey over the berries.

4. If you like mint, chop a few fresh leaves
   of it and sprinkle it over the berries.

Holiday Hickory Nut (or Butternut) Cake

8 servings

How to Separate Eggs

Inside an eggshell lies a yellow egg yolk and an egg white. When a recipe calls for an egg to be separated, it means you must separate the yolk from the white. A goal when you are separating eggs is to avoid getting any yolk mixed in with the whites. This is a little tricky, but with practice, you can do it.

To separate an egg, first wash and dry your hands. Crack the egg a little on the edge of a bowl. Working over the bowl, open the egg into 2 halves, tipping the shells a bit to let the egg white slip out and into the bowl. One of the half-shells will still contain the yolk; to get all the egg white out, carefully transfer the yolk back and forth between the 2 half-shells to let more of the egg white slide off. Put the egg yolk into a separate bowl. Be sure to remove any little pieces of eggshell that fall into either bowl.

In pioneer times making a cake with nuts in it took a lot of work. You had to gather the nuts in the woods and then crack them by hand. You had to beat the butter and sugar with a wooden spoon. You even had to build the fire in the woodstove to bake the cake! Now you can just buy hickory nuts at farmers' markets, use an electric mixer, and push a button to turn on the stove. Baking a cake still takes work, but not as much as it used to.

Hickory nuts aren't easy to crack and pick, but they're worth the effort for the flavor they bring to this cake.

Directions:

1. Heat the oven to 300 degrees. Grease the inside of a standard-sized loaf pan with oil or butter. Then sprinkle a little flour into the pan. Shake the pan to coat the bottom and sides. Dump out any extra flour.

2. Separate the 3 eggs into whites and yolks. Set them aside.

3. Whisk flour, baking powder, cinnamon, and nutmeg in a medium bowl. Set aside.

4. Place sugar and soft butter in a large bowl and beat them together until they look a little fluffy. Add milk and vanilla to the egg yolks and beat well. Stir the egg yolk mixture and flour mixture into the butter mixture. Stir in hickory nuts.

Ingredients:

Oil (or butter) and a little flour, for preparing the pan

3 large eggs

2 cups flour

1 teaspoon baking powder

1 teaspoon cinnamon

1 teaspoon nutmeg

1¼ cups sugar

1 cup (2 sticks) butter, softened to room temperature

½ cup milk

1 teaspoon vanilla extract

1 cup chopped hickory nuts or butternuts (if you don't have either of these, use pecans)

Pinch salt

2 tablespoons powdered sugar

You Will Need:

Measuring cups and spoons

Medium and large bowls

Medium loaf pan

Whisk

Electric mixer

Wooden spoons

Rubber spatula

Toothpick

Small sifter

Wire cooling rack

---

5. Add a pinch of salt to the egg whites. Using an electric mixer, beat until the whites are firm enough to form stiff peaks when you touch them. This will take several minutes.

6. Use a big spoon or rubber spatula to fold the egg whites into the cake batter. This should take a minute or two, so go slowly and be gentle! Be careful not to beat the egg whites as you fold them into the batter.

7. Spread the batter in the prepared pan. Bake for 1 hour or until a toothpick inserted in the center of the cake comes out clean.

8. Cool the cake in the loaf pan on a wire rack. When it's cool, use a small sifter to sift powdered sugar over the cake.

How to Fold Whipped Egg Whites into Cake Batter

Whipped egg whites are very delicate. They are actually made up of tiny bubbles—and as we all know, bubbles burst easily! When you fold egg whites into cake batter, you want to avoid breaking those tiny bubbles, because it's the bubbles that help make the cake rise while it's baking in the oven. So it is important to be very gentle.

To fold whipped egg whites into batter, use a large spoon or a big rubber spatula. First, place about one-quarter of the egg whites on top of the batter. Gently stir them into the batter. This will make the batter a little lighter in texture and help it mix properly with the rest of the egg whites. Now place the rest of the whipped egg whites on the batter. Don't stir or beat at this point! Instead, gently "cut" with your spoon or spatula into the egg whites and batter. When the spoon reaches the bottom of the batter, fold the batter up and over the egg whites. Turn the bowl a little and repeat the same cutting and folding motion. Keep folding the egg whites into the batter and turning the bowl until the egg whites are mixed into the batter. A few white streaks of egg white may still be showing—this is okay.

Now you are ready to bake the cake.

Maple Cream Sundaes

6–8 servings

Ingredients:

1 cup real maple syrup

1 quart vanilla ice cream or
    frozen custard

1 cup lightly salted pecans

You Will Need:

Ice cream scoop
Small serving bowls

It's hard to believe that something as sweet as maple syrup can come from the trunk of a tree. It's also amazing that people in the Wisconsin region have been enjoying maple syrup for hundreds, maybe thousands of years. It's an ancient treat that comes from the forest.

You may have had maple syrup on pancakes before, but have you ever tried it on ice cream? Although Indian children from long ago didn't know about ice cream (or milk or cows, for that matter!), they enjoyed something that tasted similar to a maple sundae. They would drizzle hot maple syrup on fresh snow. As the syrup cooled, it turned into a soft, chewy maple candy.

Directions:

To make the sundaes, scoop ice cream into cups or serving dishes. Pour some maple syrup over the ice cream. Sprinkle some pecans on top. (Oh, yum.)

At farmers' markets, you can find bottles of Wisconsin-collected pure maple syrup in all sizes.

Maple Butter Spread

About ¾ cup

Maple syrup comes from trees in a forest, while butter comes from cows on a farm. Maple syrup is a traditional ingredient for Indians, while butter is traditional to many people of European heritage. When these two very different ingredients were first combined, something new and delicious was created.

Directions:

1. Place butter and maple syrup in a large bowl.

2. Whip the mixture with an electric mixer or a whisk until the 2 ingredients are well blended.

3. Serve the spread on biscuits, pancakes, muffins, or crackers.

Ingredients:

8 tablespoons (1 stick) butter, softened to room temperature

¼ cup real maple syrup (don't use maple-flavored pancake syrup!)

Biscuits, pancakes, muffins, or crackers

You Will Need:

Large bowl
Electric mixer or a sturdy whisk

Cookee's Biscuits

10–12 small biscuits

The lumberjacks of northern Wisconsin had very big appetites. They worked hard, so they needed plenty of warm food to fuel their bodies. The logging camp cook and his assistant (called the cookee) also worked hard—to feed their hungry crew. Their day started at three o'clock in the morning, when they would begin to prepare oatmeal, hash (a cooked dish of chopped potatoes and meat), fried potatoes, fried salt pork, beans, fried cakes, pancakes, and biscuits. And all of this was just for breakfast!

Directions:

1. Heat oven to 425 degrees.

2. Combine flour, baking powder, and salt in a large bowl. Whisk to combine all the ingredients well.

3. Dump the cold butter pieces into the flour mixture. Using a pastry blender, cut the butter into the flour until the butter pieces are the size of sunflower seeds. (Or you can use a food processor for this step.)

4. Add the buttermilk. Stir the mixture with a fork until it forms a soft, lightly sticky dough. Don't overmix it or your biscuits might turn out tough.

Caution

This recipe calls for the use of a food processor, which has very sharp blades. Be sure an adult is present and watching closely when you are handling the food processor.

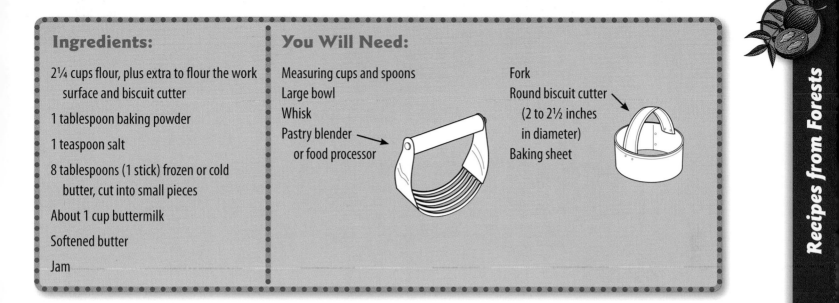

Ingredients:

2¼ cups flour, plus extra to flour the work surface and biscuit cutter

1 tablespoon baking powder

1 teaspoon salt

8 tablespoons (1 stick) frozen or cold butter, cut into small pieces

About 1 cup buttermilk

Softened butter

Jam

You Will Need:

Measuring cups and spoons
Large bowl
Whisk
Pastry blender or food processor

Fork
Round biscuit cutter (2 to 2½ inches in diameter)
Baking sheet

---

5. Sprinkle a clean countertop or table with some flour. Turn the biscuit dough out onto the floured countertop. Coat your fingers with flour and then knead the dough just a little.

6. Roll or pat the dough out to a thickness of 1 inch. Dip the biscuit cutter in flour and use it to cut the dough into rounds. Place biscuits 1 inch apart on an ungreased baking sheet. Gather the scraps of dough, press them together, and cut more biscuits until you have used all the dough.

8. Bake until raised and golden, 11–13 minutes.

9. Serve the biscuits warm with butter and jam.

How to Knead Biscuit Dough

It's fun to hold soft, squishy dough in your hands! To knead biscuit dough, fold the top half of the dough over itself, lightly press the 2 parts together, and then turn the dough a quarter turn and repeat. Keep turning, folding, and pressing for a total of 5 or 6 turns. Be gentle with the dough. Kneading the dough too much will make the biscuits tough and heavy, not tender and flaky.

Flavors from Waters and Wetlands

WHEN YOU LOOK AT A MAP of Wisconsin, you can see that we are bordered by water to the east, the west, and part of the north. From those blue boundaries, you can imagine that much Wisconsin eating has revolved around waters and wetlands (land near bodies of water). The biggest food category from these areas, of course, is fish, but people's diets in our part of the world have also included cranberries, waterfowl, and wild rice, with a few aquatic animals thrown in for good measure.

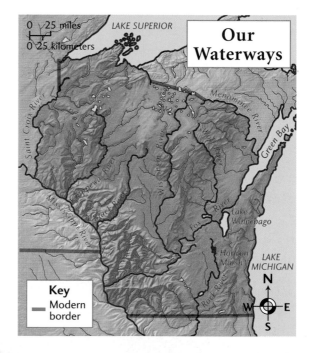

Fishing by moonlight on the Wisconsin River

Fish

Whitefish, perch, smelt. Chub, sucker, musky. Bass, pike, trout. Sturgeon, bluegill, catfish. How many of these fish have you heard of before? All these fish, plus many more types, or species, are native to Wisconsin. In this case, "native" means that they didn't come from anyplace else. These fish are Wisconsin originals.

At one time, plenty of fish swam in Wisconsin's large waterways, including Lake Michigan, Lake Superior, and the Mississippi River. Many fish also made their watery homes in the state's smaller lakes, rivers, and streams. Because so many fish could be caught easily, Wisconsin Indians ate a great deal of fish.

The Indians boiled their catch in a pot or roasted it over a fire. They also dried the fish on racks over a fire or in the sun. They stored the dried fish to eat during winter.

When pioneers from Europe came here in the 1800s, Wisconsin's rivers and lakes provided them with fish, too. The settlers salted or smoked their fish to preserve it. They made fish soup and fish cakes and prepared fish in many other ways.

The immigrants liked the fish from Wisconsin waters, but they also missed the kinds of fish they ate in their homelands. Some families had kegs of salted herring shipped to them from far away. Pickled herring was a German fish specialty. German families pickled the herring and ate it with boiled potatoes and sour cream. Norwegians enjoyed cod served in a cream sauce. Jews from Eastern Europe favored *gefilte* (pronounced guh-**fihl**-tuh) fish. They ground the fish with onions and other seasonings, shaped the mixture into balls, and boiled it. Gefilte fish is a Passover holiday treat.

Lake Superior has long been a fisherman's dream for whitefish and lake trout.

Fishing doesn't just happen in the country or on vacation. These men were fishing—in coats and ties!—on the Lake Michigan breakwater in Milwaukee around 1900.

Indian and pioneer families caught fish because they needed it for food. This is called subsistence fishing. But some people also caught fish to trade or sell. This is called commercial fishing. In the 1800s fishing companies caught and sold large amounts of fish. They shipped millions of barrels of fish by boat to sell outside of Wisconsin. Most commercial fishing occurred in Lake Michigan, Lake Superior, and the Mississippi River.

Commercial fishermen needed to pack fish in ice if they were shipping it fresh. Before refrigerators were invented, people cut chunks of ice from frozen lakes and streams. They used ice to keep food cold in kitchen "ice boxes" and underground cellars. Business owners, such as beer makers and butchers, also needed ice to keep their products cold. Wisconsin was a good place to get ice, because of its cold winters and clean waterways. During the late 1800s, ice harvesting was a booming business in Wisconsin. Workers used special saws to cut giant "ice cakes" from the frozen waters. The cakes weighed two hundred pounds or more! They were packed into nearby storage buildings or shipped to Chicago or Milwaukee on trains.

This painting shows Menominee fishermen spearfishing by torchlight long ago.

Ice harvesting was a huge industry here in the years before refrigeration.

Commercial fishermen supply fish for fish fries all around the state.

Commercial fishing was an important industry for many years. Wisconsin was one of the leading states for commercial fishing. But then problems arose. Commercial fishing became *too* successful. The companies caught so many fish that the fish population decreased a great deal. Also, large factories dumped garbage and waste into the Great Lakes. This dumping polluted the waters and destroyed more fish. Another problem was non-native fish that made their way into Wisconsin waters. The non-native fish got in when a large canal was built to let ships into the Great Lakes. This canal was called the Welland Canal. The Welland Canal let in non-native fish along with ships. Some of these non-native fish, like the sea lamprey, killed the native fish.

By the middle of the 1900s, the problems in Wisconsin waters were very serious. The government passed laws to limit the number of fish that people could catch. More laws were passed to prevent water pollution. The new laws helped but didn't solve all the problems.

Going fishing and eating fish are important traditions in Wisconsin. Most people who catch fish no longer need it as their main food source. Yet going fishing is still a pleasant pastime or hobby. (Fishing as a pastime is called sport fishing.)

Today we are still trying to find the best ways to keep our waterways healthy and full of fish. That way we can continue to enjoy catching and eating fish.

Musky Caught At Ross's Teal Lake Resort Hayward Wis.

Ross's Teal Lake Lodge near Hayward has been hosting vacationing families for more than 100 years.

Fish Boils

Door County is a 75-mile peninsula surrounded by the waters of Green Bay on the west and Lake Michigan on the east, with lots of shoreline and more lighthouses than any other county in the United States. Being surrounded by that much water meant that shipping and sailing were important in the county's early development. Fishing also has provided both jobs and delicious food to the area.

Fish boils are one of Door County's major attractions for visitors, and many restaurants feature fish boils, especially on summer weekends. The ingredients for a fish boil are really simple: Start with a large kettle of salted water above a blazing bonfire. The chef or boil master checks to see if the temperature is hot enough and then drops in potatoes and sometimes onions. A bit later, the boil master adds large chunks of Lake Michigan whitefish. What makes a fish boil really boil hard—and what makes it exciting to watch—is the kerosene added to the fire after the ingredients are in the pot. The fire then blazes up, and some of the water boils over and out. Then the fish is ready to be served, with the onions and potatoes on the side, all under a coat of melted butter. Most Door County fish boil meals also include rye bread, coleslaw, and a slice of Door County cherry pie.

The "boil-over" is the most exciting part of a fish boil.

Fish boils like this are one of the most popular tourist attractions in Door County.

Waterfowl and Freshwater Animals

Centuries ago, there were so many ducks, geese, and other waterfowl that they seemed to fill the sky. Wetlands were also crowded with beavers, frogs, turtles, opossums, and many more kinds of water-loving animals. These wild creatures supplied food for the Indians, explorers, and fur traders of long ago.

Can you imagine what beaver tail would taste like? The French voyageurs who explored the Wisconsin region during the 1600s thought beaver tail was a tasty treat. Jean Nicolet was probably the first non-Indian to come to Wisconsin. He must have been happy when Ho-Chunk chiefs invited him to a feast—where they served 120 beavers at the meal!

Native people and early explorers hunted beavers for their fur pelts as well as for their meat.

Pioneers also hunted wild ducks, geese, and other freshwater fare. Some families raised geese and ducks on their farms, too. They often served the waterfowl with vegetables from their farm gardens. During the holidays, children loved roast goose almost as much as their Christmas gifts.

Some Indians hunted waterfowl and other wild game to trade with pioneer families. The farmers gave the Indians cheese and butter in exchange for the game.

Waterfowl and freshwater animals eventually became harder to find, especially in southern Wisconsin, where so many pioneers settled. Today, few people eat such foods as turtle soup or fried frog legs. But people still eat duck or goose from the grocery store or in a restaurant. And many still go hunting for food in the wetlands of Wisconsin.

Families have enjoyed duck hunting in Wisconsin for generations.

Wild rice is an ancient Indian food. Long ago, it thrived in many parts of Wisconsin. It was a very important part of the diet to the Indians in the area. One of the tribes, the Menominee, even took its name from the Indian word for wild rice: *manomin* (pronounced mah-**no**-min).

Wild rice looks like large, dark-brown rice, but it is not related to brown or white rice. Wild rice is the cereal grain, or seed, of a tall grass plant that grows in marshes and along the shores of lakes and slow-moving streams in North America. Wild rice ripens in late summer to early autumn. It has a nutty flavor and a chewy texture.

In this illustration drawn in the mid-1800s, Indian women harvest wild rice.

At harvest time, Indians moved their villages to "rice camps" on lakeshores. Each family sent two people out in a canoe. One person used a long pole to move the canoe through the rice beds. Then the other person used two sticks to harvest the rice. One stick would bend the rice stalks over the canoe. The other stick would knock the ripe grains into the bottom of the canoe.

When the canoe was full of wild rice, the Indians returned to their rice camp. First, they cleaned off the rice. Then they dried it in the sun or parched it over fires. Parching helped loosen the outer husks from the grains of wild rice. It also gave the rice a toasty flavor.

Wild rice beds are still important sources of nutritious food for Wisconsin's Native people.

Next, the Indians tramped on the rice, to loosen the husks even more. This was called dancing the rice.

An Ojibwe man harvests wild rice on the Bad River Indian Reservation. He is doing it in the traditional way—just like the women in the early print on page 43.

After that, they winnowed the wild rice to get the loosened husks off the grains. To winnow, they put the rice on large trays made of birchbark. Then they flipped the rice into the air. The husks, or chaff, blew away in the breeze, and the rice fell back onto the tray.

Finally, the wild rice could be cooked and eaten. Indians prepared it in many ways. Sometimes they boiled wild rice with deer fat, or with corn, beans, or squash. Sometimes they added maple syrup for seasoning.

Wild rice takes a lot of work, but it is very nutritious. It can also be stored for a long time. Indians depended on the wild rice harvest to feed them during winter.

When white settlers arrived and began to clear the land for farming, many natural wild rice beds were destroyed. As farms, towns, and cities grew in number, more Indian wild rice beds were lost.

During the 1960s, farmers began to grow wild rice in large paddies. A paddy is a rice field that grows in shallow water. Paddy-raised rice is harvested and processed with machines to get it ready to eat.

True wild rice is gathered and processed by hand. This takes longer so true wild rice is more expensive, but it also tastes especially wonderful. Harvesting wild rice by hand is also a meaningful tradition and a valuable source of income for Indians today.

The cranberry is Wisconsin's official state fruit. Wisconsin growers raise more cranberries than any other fruit. They harvest more cranberries than any other state. In 2009 Wisconsin produced nearly four million bushels of cranberries.

How did the little red cranberry become so important in Wisconsin?

Cranberries started as a wild food. They grew in marshes, or wetlands, in many parts of the region. This "marsh berry" was well known by most Indians before Wisconsin became a state. Indians gathered ripe berries in the fall and ate them fresh or dried in many kinds of preparations. The Menominee tribe mixed cranberries with corn, for example, and the Ojibwe used them to make tea.

Indians also traded or sold baskets of wild berries to non-Indian travelers and immigrants. The new settlers enjoyed the taste of this fruit. They learned that cranberries are very nutritious, too. Cranberries helped them stay healthy in their new land.

Settlers soon began to gather cranberries to sell, as the Indians did. They also decided to grow cranberries, instead of just gathering wild ones.

Members of the Ho-Chunk tribe have been harvesting cranberries in Wisconsin for centuries.

Wisconsin is the number one cranberry-growing state in the country.

Cranberries don't grow on trees, like some fruits. Instead they grow on vines in bogs. Think of a bog as a kind of marsh, or wet field. Cranberry crops can freeze if the fruit doesn't get ripe before the first frost comes. That means the first cranberry growers needed a way to protect their crops from early frost.

In 1860 Edward Sacket came to Berlin, Wisconsin, and decided to grow cranberries. He copied growing methods that he had seen in the northeastern part of the United States. Sacket had ditches dug in the Wisconsin marshlands that he owned. He planted cranberry vines in the ditches. When the weather got cold, he could flood the ditches with water from nearby streams. This kept the vines warmer and helped prevent frost damage to the cranberries.

At that time people didn't have TV or the Internet to give them the weather forecast, but farmers learned other ways to predict when frost was coming. Some even had access to telegraphs—a system for sending messages over wire or radio—that gave them weather reports. Sacket and other cranberry growers learned ways to prevent frost damage. For example, some set out huge iron pans filled with flaming tar to keep the vines warm.

What's in a Name?

Cranberries were known by different names, but the name that lasted came from the words *crane berry*. Cranes are large birds that often live near bogs and eat wild cranberries. Some people called the fruit crane berries because they thought the plant's blossom looked like the head of a crane. *Crane berry* got shortened to *cranberry*, and that's how the cranberry got its name.

Cranberries are delicious and highly nutritious, too!

Edward Sacket's bogs were very successful. He started a cranberry-growing boom in the state. By the late 1800s, cranberries were big business in Wisconsin, especially in Jackson, Juneau, Monroe, and Wood Counties. That's when the state worked to become the largest cranberry producer in the nation. In the 1890s, growers in Wood County asked the railroads to post frost warnings in the windows of trains passing through their cranberry areas. Then, if cold weather was coming, the growers had time to prepare.

Most Wisconsin cranberries were sold as a fresh fruit until the 1980s and 1990s. Today, mechanized equipment makes harvesting cranberries easier and faster. Now, only a small part of Wisconsin's cranberry crop is sold fresh. Most of it is made into cranberry juice, dried cranberries, and other cranberry products.

Baked Whitefish

5–6 servings

Fishermen show off their catch.

Fish was very important in the diet of Indian tribes who lived near the Great Lakes. The Great Lakes were home to the whitefish, a large, mild-tasting fish. The Ojibwe often boiled whitefish, or they roasted it over an open flame.

European immigrants learned about whitefish when they settled in the region. It was a new kind of fish for them, and they began to prepare it many ways. Sometimes they boiled large amounts of it at church picnics and other community gatherings.

Here is an easy way to prepare whitefish today. You can bake a small or large amount of it. If it's frozen you can thaw it before baking it, or not. But if you don't thaw it, it will take a few minutes longer to cook.

Directions:

1. Heat the oven to 425 degrees. Line a large baking dish with parchment paper or aluminum foil.

2. Place the fish filets, with the skin side down, in the baking dish.

3. Cut the lemon in half. Use a lemon juicer to juice the lemon halves. (Or cut the lemon into quarters and just squeeze the quarters really hard over a bowl.) Discard the seeds.

4. Sprinkle lemon juice evenly over the fish—about 2 or 3 teaspoons for each filet.

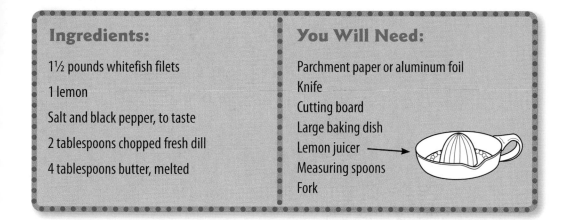

Ingredients:

1½ pounds whitefish filets

1 lemon

Salt and black pepper, to taste

2 tablespoons chopped fresh dill

4 tablespoons butter, melted

You Will Need:

Parchment paper or aluminum foil

Knife

Cutting board

Large baking dish

Lemon juicer

Measuring spoons

Fork

5. Sprinkle some salt, pepper, and fresh dill evenly over the fish.

6. Spoon the melted butter evenly over the fish—about 2 to 3 teaspoons for each filet.

7. Bake the fish until it looks creamy white all the way through the flesh (poke into the fish with a fork to check). This will take about 10–15 minutes. Serve the fish right away, while it's nice and hot.

Lots of Wisconsin families head "up north" for fishing vacations.

Fish Chowder

6–8 servings

Ingredients:

2–4 slices bacon, chopped

⅓ cup diced onion

1¾ cups water or chicken broth

1½ cups diced potatoes

½ teaspoon salt

⅛ teaspoon black pepper

1 pound walleyed pike or other fish, cut into small chunks

3 cups whole or low-fat milk

1 tablespoon chopped fresh parsley

You Will Need:

Sharp knife

Cutting board

Measuring cups and spoons

Soup pot or large saucepan with lid

Wooden spoons

One of the ways that German immigrants prepared fish was to make soup out of it. They added bacon to the soup to give it a special smoky flavor, plus herbs from their gardens.

Directions:

1. Cook the bacon in a soup pot over medium-high heat. Stir it once in a while as it cooks. Cook until the bacon pieces are brown. This will take about 6–8 minutes.

2. Add the onions and let them cook for 3–4 minutes. Give them a stir once or twice while they cook.

3. Stir in the water or broth, potatoes, salt, and pepper. Let the mixture come to a simmer (slow, low bubbling), then turn the heat down to low. Cover the pot. Let the soup simmer until the potatoes are tender (to test this, you can cool a potato off and taste it, or you can pierce one with a fork to make sure it is soft all the way through). This will take about 10–15 minutes.

4. Add the fish chunks and let them simmer 5 minutes.

5. Add the milk. Heat the soup until it is hot (but do not let it boil).

6. Stir in the parsley. You can serve the soup right away. Or, turn it off and let it stand for 30–60 minutes—it will gain flavor this way. Reheat it before serving.

Smoked Fish Cream Cheese Spread

2–3 cups

Indians and white settlers smoked fish over a slow-burning fire. This was a way to preserve the fish so it could be eaten at a later time. Today we have refrigerators and freezers to preserve fish, but we still enjoy the taste of smoked fish.

You can buy smoked fish spread at a fish market or grocery store, but it's also fun to make your own. Spread the smoked fish mixture on crackers or use it as a dip for carrot sticks.

Directions:

1. Remove the skin and **all** the bones from the smoked fish.

2. Put the fish in a medium-sized bowl. Use your fingers to work through the fish to break it up. Look carefully for any other bones and remove them.

3. Rinse the green onions. Chop them into tiny pieces.

4. Use a fork to mix the green onions, cream cheese, and milk into the fish until everything is well combined.

Ingredients:

- 1 pound chunk of smoked lake trout, salmon, or whitefish
- 3 or 4 green onions
- 1 package (8 ounces) cream cheese, softened to room temperature
- 1–2 tablespoons milk

You Will Need:

Medium bowl	Sharp knife
Cutting board	Fork
Measuring spoons	

How to Debone Fish

Smoked fish often has many tiny bones that are hard to see. To get the bones out, peel off the skin all around the fish—the skin will come off easily in large pieces. The bones lie under the meat on both sides of the fish. Use a fork or your finger and work on one side of the fish at a time. Gently pull the meat in pieces from the top edge to the bottom edge of the fish. Some of the meat will come off in big pieces, and some in small pieces. Carefully check each piece for bones and pull them out, then place the boneless pieces in a bowl. After you've finished both sides of the fish, go through the bowl of fish and check once more for bones. Wrap up all the bones and skin in newspaper and discard it.

Before you use the fish in a recipe, be sure an adult checks the fish carefully to make sure that all the bones have been removed.

Duck with Door County Cherries

4 servings

Wisconsin's waters have been home to ducks, geese, coots (small, black ducklike waterbirds), and other kinds of waterfowl for a very long time. Hunting for waterfowl was a common practice in past centuries. It is still a tradition in many families today. Hunting is one way we can get food as our ancestors did—not from the grocery store, but from nature. Do you know anyone who goes duck hunting?

This recipe is adapted with permission from *Wisconsin Wild Foods: 100 Recipes for Badger State Bounties,* by John Motoviloff (Trails Books). It tastes great served with wild rice, another food that comes from Wisconsin waterways.

Directions:

1. Heat the oven to 350 degrees.

2. Combine the flour, salt, and pepper in a paper bag. Shake the bag to mix everything up.

3. Place the duck breasts in the bag. Shake the bag until the meat is coated all over with the flour mixture.

Ingredients:

1 cup flour

2 teaspoons salt

1 teaspoon black pepper

2 boneless duck breasts (with skin on),
    each about 8–10 ounces

2 tablespoons butter

2 cups Door County frozen, pitted tart or
    sweet cherries (with their juices)

You Will Need:

Paper bag

Measuring cups and spoons

Large skillet

Tongs for turning the duck

Medium baking dish with cover
    (or use aluminum foil to cover)

Wooden spoon

4. Melt the butter in a large skillet over medium-high heat. When the butter is bubbly (but before it turns brown!), add the duck pieces to the pan. Let them brown on the first side for 3–5 minutes. Then turn them over and brown them on the other side for 3–5 minutes longer.

5. Turn the heat down to medium.

6. Remove the duck pieces from the skillet and place them in a baking dish (one that is just big enough to fit the pieces). Set the baking dish aside.

7. Stir the cherries into the skillet. Use a wooden spoon to scrape all around the bottom of the skillet. This will get all the delicious little bits that are there into the cherries. Cook the cherries for 10 minutes, stirring occasionally.

8. Pour the cherries over the duck. Cover the baking dish with a lid or aluminum foil. Bake the duck until it is tender, about 45–60 minutes.

Wild Rice with Egg Strips

4–6 servings

Wild rice is a traditional food for Indians. Here is a delicious way to enjoy it.

Ingredients:

3 cups water

1 cup uncooked wild rice, rinsed in cold water and drained

1½ teaspoons salt, divided

4 eggs

2 tablespoons finely chopped fresh chives

¼ teaspoon black pepper

2 tablespoon butter or olive oil

You Will Need:

Measuring cups and spoons
Medium saucepan with lid
Medium bowl
Whisk or fork
Nonstick skillet
Spatula
Cutting board
Knife

Directions:

1. Place water, wild rice, and 1 teaspoon of the salt in a saucepan. Give it a stir. Place the saucepan over medium heat.

2. Let the mixture come to a boil, then lower the heat and partially cover the pan so that the wild rice simmers slowly. Let the wild rice cook until all the water is gone and the wild rice is tender. This should take 25–35 minutes. If it's not tender when all the water is gone, add a little more water and keep cooking until the wild rice is tender.

3. While the wild rice is cooking, crack the eggs into a bowl. Add chives, pepper, and ½ teaspoon salt. Use a whisk or a fork to beat the eggs until smooth.

4. Put the butter or oil in a nonstick skillet over medium heat. When the butter starts to bubble, pour in the eggs. Don't stir. Let the eggs cook like a pancake for a couple of minutes.

5. After 2 or 3 minutes, the egg pancake will look cooked all around the edges and should be browned on the bottom. Use a spatula to loosen it from the pan. Flip the egg pancake over and brown the other side.

6. Take the egg pancake out of the skillet and place it on a cutting board. Cut it into strips. Add the egg strips to the cooked wild rice, and serve.

Wild Rice Pudding with Dried Cherries

6 servings

Try making this breakfast pudding with other kinds of dried fruit besides cherries, such as raisins or dried cranberries.

Directions:

1. Heat oven to 350 degrees. Use a paper towel to butter the baking dish with the softened butter.

2. Crack eggs into a large bowl. Add half-and-half, maple syrup, and cinnamon. Whisk until smooth.

3. Stir in the dried cherries and wild rice. Spoon mixture into the prepared baking dish.

4. Bake until the liquid is gone and the pudding looks only a little moist. This will take 35–40 minutes. Let stand for 10–15 minutes before serving.

5. If you wish, add a dollop of yogurt alongside each serving.

Ingredients:

1 tablespoon butter, softened

3 large eggs

1 cup half-and-half

⅓ cup real maple syrup

1 teaspoon ground cinnamon

¾ cup dried cherries

3 cups cooked and cooled wild rice

Vanilla yogurt (optional)

You Will Need:

Measuring cups and spoons
Paper towel
An 8-by-12-inch baking dish
Large bowl
Whisk
Mixing spoon

Fresh Cranberry Relish

8 servings

Ingredients:

2 seedless oranges

1 pound fresh cranberries

1 cup sugar

You Will Need:

Sharp knife

Cutting board

Measuring cup

Food processor (If you don't have
one, you can chop the fruit with a
knife. That is how pioneers did it!)

Rubber spatula

Caution

This recipe calls for the use of a
food processor, which has very
sharp blades. Be sure an adult
is present and watching closely
when you are handling
the food processor.

How can you tell if a cranberry is fresh? See if it bounces! Early settlers dropped cranberries to sort the good ones from the bad ones. If they sprang back when dropped, the cranberries were pronounced first-rate. Even today, cranberries are given a "bounce test" before they are packaged for sale. Try the bounce test on your cranberries. A really fresh cranberry will bounce four or more inches high. How fresh are your cranberries?

This recipe for cranberry relish makes a wonderful side dish for Thanksgiving turkey. But it's also good with chicken or pork, or on crackers, or just eaten on its own! Try some on a turkey sandwich with mayonnaise and lettuce.

Directions:

1. Rinse the oranges. With the peels still on, cut each one into 8 pieces.

2. Fit the metal blade into a food processor. Place orange pieces, cranberries, and sugar in the bowl of the food processor. Secure the top on the food processor.

3. Turn the pulse button on and off until all the fruit is finely chopped. You might have to stop the machine once or twice to scrape down the sides of the work bowl.

4. Scrape the fruit mixture into a serving bowl. Let the mixture stand for 20–30 minutes to let the sugar dissolve completely. Stir it once in a while during this time. Then cover and refrigerate the relish until serving time.

Cranberry Raspberry Smoothie

6–8 servings

You can add whole cranberries or raspberries to this smoothie if you like. They can be fresh or thawed. Just blend them with the other ingredients. Other berries or fruits could go in it, too. Experiment and see what you like!

Directions:

Pour the juice and the yogurt into a blender. Put the lid on tight. Blend until smooth. If you want to make a thinner smoothie, add a couple tablespoons of milk and blend again.

Ingredients:

2 cups cranberry-raspberry juice

2 containers (6 ounces each) raspberry yogurt

Milk (optional)

You Will Need:

Measuring cup
Blender

The machine in the front of this photograph sorts cranberries. The one in the background puts them through the bounce test.

Cranberry Pecan Cookies

36–40 cookies

These cookies are golden and chewy. They contain fresh cranberries, which are available in autumn, when cranberries ripen.

Ingredients:

8 tablespoons (1 stick) butter, softened to room temperature

1 cup white sugar

1 cup brown sugar

⅓ cup milk

1 large egg

3 cups flour

1 teaspoon baking powder

½ teaspoon baking soda

1 teaspoon salt

2½ cups fresh cranberries

1 cup pecans

You Will Need:

2 large cookie sheets
Parchment paper (optional)
Electric mixer (optional)
Whisk
Wooden spoon
Measuring cups and spoons
Large and medium mixing bowls
Cutting board
Sharp knife
Spatula
Wire cooling rack

Directions:

1. Heat oven to 350 degrees.

2. Grease 2 large cookie sheets or line them with parchment paper.

3. Place butter, white sugar, and brown sugar in a big bowl. Use a wooden spoon or an electric mixer to beat the ingredients until creamy. Then beat in the milk and egg.

4. Place flour, baking powder, baking soda, and salt in another bowl. Use a whisk to combine them well.

5. Using a knife, chop the cranberries and pecans into smaller pieces.

6. Stir the flour mixture, cranberries, and pecans into the butter mixture until everything is combined.

7. Place heaping teaspoonfuls of the dough in rows onto the cookie sheets. The cookies should be about 2 inches apart.

8. Bake the cookies until they are golden, 12–15 minutes. Watch the first batch closely to get the right amount of time to bake the second batch.

9. Let the cookies cool on the pan for a few minutes, then use a spatula to transfer them to a wire rack to cool all the way.

Mulled Cranberry Orange Drink

5–6 servings

A mulled beverage is one that is heated and spiced. It can be made with cranberry juice, apple cider, or other fruit juices. In pioneer days, Scandinavians and other immigrants mulled wine. They served it as a festive beverage during the holidays. Does your family drink any hot beverages during the holidays?

Directions:

1. Rinse and dry the oranges.

2. Grate the zest (that's the outer, orange-colored part of the peel) off 2 of the oranges. Put the grated peel in a pot. Cut the oranges in half and squeeze the juice into the pot. Slice the third orange into thin rounds.

3. Add the cranberry juice drink, cinnamon stick pieces, and honey to the pot. Bring the mixture to a low simmer. Cover and cook for about 5 minutes.

4. Ladle the drink into cups. Add an orange slice to each cup and serve.

Ingredients:

3 large seedless oranges, divided

4 cups bottled cranberry juice drink

3 cinnamon sticks, broken into pieces

3 tablespoons honey

You Will Need:

Cloth or paper towels
Grater
Large pot with lid
Measuring spoons
Lemon juicer
Ladle for serving

Flavors from Fields and Orchards

WE ENJOY MANY FOODS that come from commercial growers, the farmers who grow vegetable, fruit, and grain crops to sell to others—that is, for market. Successful farmers who make a living from the land know that the kinds of crops they grow depend on the soil on their farms, the rainfall, and the length of the growing season where they live.

Our state's different physical regions also have very different soils, different amounts of rainfall, and different lengths of growing seasons. These variations affected the way Native people got the food they needed to survive during the thousands of years before non-Indians arrived in the area that became Wisconsin. In the northern part of the state, growing seasons were shorter, and the soils supported large forests. Native people who lived in the north relied more heavily on the forests and waters for most of their diet: wild rice, waterfowl, fish, venison and other meats, and maple sugar. Native people in the southern part of Wisconsin had rich prairie soil and longer growing seasons. These Indians became Wisconsin's first farmers, with gardens of corn, beans, and squash. Of course, they also hunted and fished, ate cranberries and other berries, and gathered nuts.

From the height of the corn, it looks like this is a midsummer field!

When Wheat Was King

By 1836, enough non-Indians had settled in the area to form the Wisconsin Territory, and in 1848, Wisconsin became the 30th state. Most of the farmers who pioneered here around that time settled in a wide belt of land that stretched from the southeast along Lake Michigan to the northwest along the Mississippi River. Settlers who came to farm found that wheat was easy to grow in the fertile prairie soil. Wheat put daily bread on pioneer tables.

Farmers worked with simple handheld tools, oxen or horses, and steel plows, but nothing that needed a motor. When tractors and other mechanized farm equipment became available in the late 1800s, farming changed. Now farmers were able to plant more acres of land. Prairies in southern and western Wisconsin became fields of wheat. By 1860, Wisconsin ranked second only to Illinois as the nation's top wheat-producing state.

The first settlers who came to Wisconsin used handheld tools like this shovel plow to get the soil ready for planting.

These farmers harvested wheat with handheld tools, in the days before big farm equipment did the work.

More settlers came to farm, and they too found wheat easy to grow. But the wheat boom did not last long. Wheat used up too many nutrients and wore out the soil after just a few seasons. Farmland that was once fertile stopped producing as much as it had in the past. Many wheat farmers decided to try their luck on the much larger prairies on the Great Plains west of Wisconsin.

When more wheat was grown on the Great Plains, the wheat farmers who remained in Wisconsin earned less for their crops. Then from 1864 to 1866, chinch bugs became a kind of plague that quickly and completely ate up most of the state's remaining wheat crop.

But wheat was never the only crop grown in Wisconsin. The farmers who remained and the new farmers who arrived and planned to stay in the state wanted to keep their soil fertile and their fields full of healthy crops. They had to experiment to see which crops would do best on their land.

Someone must have been mighty proud of this new plow. All the neighbors have come to see it.

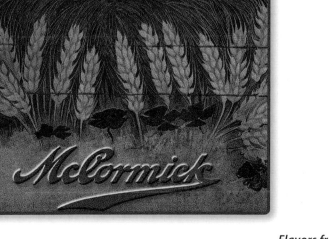

A lush, golden field of wheat adorns the cover of this 1905 farm-machinery catalog.

Many Farms, Many Crops

Dairy farming and feed crops (crops such as corn, oats, and hay that farmers feed their animals) replaced wheat and suited the soil and climate of much, but not all, of Wisconsin. Most of the central and northern counties have a cooler climate and sandy soil, which do not work well for dairy farms. These counties stretch from Door in the east across the central plains of Portage, Waupaca, Juneau, Adams, and their neighbors, plus Chippewa, Barron, and Dunn Counties in the northwest. Fields in those places have been excellent for growing many kinds of fruits and vegetables. Non-Indian farming families arrived in all of these counties later than did the farmers who settled in the southern counties or in those that bordered the Mississippi River or Lakes Michigan and Superior.

Wisconsin farm families often planted "kitchen gardens" of vegetables and herbs for their own use. But many of the vegetables grown in these gardens soon outgrew their original plots. As more people moved to towns and cities where they were no longer able to grow their own vegetables, farmers realized they could make money raising vegetable crops for market in those towns and cities.

Even before Wisconsin became a state, potatoes were the biggest cash crop. More than 150 years later, Wisconsin remains a leading potato producer. In 2005, Wisconsin ranked third in the United States in the number of pounds of potatoes harvested. The central "sand counties" (so called because of the sandy soil) are big potato producers, but potatoes are grown in other areas of the state as well.

In this central Wisconsin potato field in the early 1900s, the whole family—and even the dog—got in on the harvest.

Hop to It

Did you know that there are flowers in beer? It's true. Brewers add the blossoms of hop plants to beer in order to give it a pleasant bitterness. Hops were an important crop in Wisconsin during the 1860s for two reasons. First, many beer-loving German immigrants lived in the state. They needed hops to make their own beer. Second, insects had taken over most of the hops farms in the eastern states. That meant people from those states also needed hops grown in the young state of Wisconsin.

Hops provided jobs for many people, especially in Waukesha and Sauk Counties. In 1867 Sauk County alone grew 20 percent of the nation's hops. Some families there got very rich from their hops crops. But soon many other growers were raising hops, and the hops farms in the eastern states recovered from the insects. Having so much hops available meant that the price of the crop dropped. Wisconsin farmers found they could no longer make enough money growing hops. And the state never again had so many successful hops farms.

But recently, Wisconsin farmers have decided to give hops another try. Beer makers need more hops, so perhaps hops will be a popular crop once again.

Hops are a climbing plant. Look at how tall these ones in Sauk County grew!

By the 1900s, Wisconsin's farmers were already leading growers of potatoes, peas, beans, cabbage, cranberries, and cherries. These fruits and vegetables remind us that our state has a wide range of land types. Crops need to be selected to suit all kinds of land. Growing many kinds of crops is known as crop diversity.

Remember that season after season of planting wheat had worn out the soil. Other crops that are planted in the same field year after year also wear out the soil. Farmers learned to rotate crops. That is, they planted a different crop in the field from season to season. For example, a field planted in corn one year would be planted in alfalfa the next year. Farmers came to understand that soil likes having different crops grown in it. Changes in crops help the soil remain fertile. Peas are a crop that works well in rotation, because they enrich the soil.

THE KIND WE RAISE AT ABBOTSFORD, WIS.

"Tall tales" postcards like this one, in which the photographer used camera tricks to make the potatoes look huge, were popular in the early 1900s.

Students at Union High School in Livingston, Wisconsin, displayed these vegetables at the school's agricultural fair in 1912.

Canned Peas, Please!

Peas are second only to potatoes in Wisconsin agricultural history. Canning peas for shipping and storing helped make this crop very important to Wisconsin agriculture. In fact, the canning industry in the state began when Albert Landreth of Manitowoc County began experimenting with canning peas in 1883. Three years later, he opened his first cannery in Manitowoc. Just a few years after that, the county was one of the nation's top producers of peas.

These women were inspecting peas at a Wisconsin cannery in the 1970s.

By the early 1900s, 21 canneries around the state provided new jobs for many local people. For example, workers in Burlington and Platteville canned corn and tomatoes, while workers in Randolph also canned peas and pickles. Seasonal workers, known as migrants, came to the state to work in canneries. This was especially true in the eastern and central counties of the state. Some migrant families settled permanently in Wisconsin. Diversity in crops encouraged the growing diversity of Wisconsin people as groups of newcomers moved into farming communities.

As people from different cultures and backgrounds moved into Wisconsin, other forms of agriculture developed in many areas around the state. Both spearmint and peppermint grow well in Wisconsin, and these are used in products like candy and toothpaste. Some farms produce ginseng—a root particularly valued for its uses in medicines—and other farms produce honey, beef cattle, chickens, or pigs. All of these products are important to Wisconsin's economy.

Colorful Orchards

Apples are one of the oldest of Wisconsin's fruit harvests. And since the state has so many apples, they also make for one of our *biggest* fruit harvests. Given our harsh climate and short growing season, only the hardiest apples thrive here. The biggest apple-producing areas in the state are near Gays Mills in Crawford County and in Bayfield, Door, and Milwaukee Counties. What do these areas have in common? Some, like Crawford County, tend to have rolling hills. Other counties are close to Lake Superior or Lake Michigan. Both hills and nearness to the Great Lakes provide some protection from killing frosts. About 300 kinds of apples are grown in the state, and you can find them at farmers' markets and fruit stands each autumn—including many varieties that you could never find in grocery stores!

One of the nicest things about apples is that there are earlier and later harvest times, so you can experiment with different apple flavors throughout the fall. Early apples begin to ripen in late July and include the Jersey Mac and the Paula Red. Later in the season you can move on to Honeycrisp, Spartan, Empire, and Fireside. Just before Halloween, you can try Jonathan, Golden Delicious, Golden Russet, and Ida Red. And this list includes only 10 of those 300 varieties.

Golden Delicious apples are one of the many varieties grown in Wisconsin.

Tart cherries (also called pie cherries) are another favorite orchard crop. While cherry trees can be seen growing here and there around the state, only Door County is famous for its many cherry orchards. Why? The Door Peninsula is practically surrounded by water. One shore faces the waters of Green Bay. The tip and opposite shore face Lake Michigan. These big bodies of water make the climate mild in winter. The air warms slowly and steadily in spring, protecting the cherries from late frosts and letting them grow slowly. As happens during apple harvest time, many families and tourists stop at orchards that offer "pick your own" harvesting. And some people think that a trip to Door County is not complete until they've eaten a yummy slice of fresh cherry pie. You can also often find canned, frozen, and dried Door County cherries in grocery stores all over the state, so you can enjoy them year-round.

Cherry picking requires careful hands!

Cherries in bloom in Door County

Eating Locally

In the later years of the 20th century, people around Wisconsin and the rest of the United States began worrying more about the health of citizens, both children and adults. Too many people were sitting too much of the time, eating too much snack food and too many sweets, drinking too much soda, and making other unhealthy choices. People began to realize that they should be more active and make better and healthier food choices. Such choices include eating more locally grown fruits and vegetables. These local fruits and vegetables tend to be fresher and richer in nutrients than food that comes from far away or that has been heavily processed to make it last longer.

At about the same time that people were realizing that local food is often healthier food, many were also beginning to understand that buying local food helps our environment, supports small farmers, and puts more money into our local businesses. And then there are those who feel that the best reason of all to eat locally raised food is that it *tastes* fresher and better!

Since the 1990s, local farmers' markets have played a major role in this trend toward taking better care of ourselves and the world around us. Farmers' markets are not new. Since the mid-1800s, some cities have had markets where farmers can sell their produce during the growing season.

Hmong farmers display their weekly harvests at the Dane County Farmers' Market in Madison.

What's a CSA?

Another way that Wisconsin families have supported local farmers is by becoming a partner in a farm through a program known as community-supported agriculture (CSA). CSAs began in Germany, Switzerland, and Japan in the 1960s and got started in Wisconsin in the late 1980s. When people join CSAs, they become members of a particular farm. They invest their money in a "share" of whatever the farm produces during a growing season. Then each week, they receive a box of fresh produce. Some farms allow members to pay for part of their share by going to the farm and helping with the harvesting, cleaning, or packing of produce each week. Families who join CSAs feel that they are connecting to the farm families, their land, and their harvests. And they enjoy getting different fresh foods every week.

It's fun to see what's been harvested when you pick up your CSA box each week!

But now that people are trying to support eating locally grown and produced food, families all over the state can find farmers' markets near them. Local farmers sell their produce around the Iron County Courthouse in Hurley during growing season just as they do around the state capitol in Madison. Many farmers' markets, like those in West Allis and Madison, allow only those farmers who raise everything they sell to set up their booths at the market.

Farmers' markets help people buy more locally grown fruits and vegetables. But that's not the only way people in cities get fresh produce. Milwaukee is one of the cities in the United States where you can find urban farms—small plots of land used for commercial cultivation right in the city—like the one Will Allen operates. This former professional basketball player is a leader in the urban farming movement in Wisconsin and across the country.

Will Allen's organization is known as Growing Power, and it is located in what he calls a "food desert"—a neighborhood with many poor or low-income people and no grocery store close by. Growing Power provides many healthy choices for people who did not have places that offered such choices before.

Will Allen always has his sleeves rolled up and is ready to work at Growing Power on the northwest side of Milwaukee.

Will Allen was raised on a farm. After his basketball career ended, he missed working the land. He became an organic farmer on his farm just south of Milwaukee. Organic farmers like Will use natural methods to control pests and to make their farm soil as productive as possible. They do not use human-made chemicals such as fertilizers and weed killers in their soil. Many people believe that organic farming is healthier for people, animals, and the environment. Will opened a small store to sell vegetables from his farm, and he hired local teenagers to help. When one group of students asked if Will could help them start a garden, he decided to grow food closer to the people who needed it.

Will also wanted to teach people how to grow food themselves in cities where there was little space to do so. To accomplish this goal, he began developing good soil, because the better the soil, the more food you can grow in a limited space. Will Allen developed good soil by composting—which means combining food scraps with yard waste such as leaves and grass clippings and letting them decay. The crumbly, dark mixture that results is called compost. Farmers and gardeners use compost to enrich soil. Growers like Will Allen also use worms for composting. Worms make super composters because as they wiggle through the soil, they help break down the food scraps into tiny bits. It may seem funny, but worm poop makes terrific fertilizer, so hooray for red wigglers!

Summer vegetables aren't just healthful, they're beautiful, too!

Growing strong and healthy bodies means eating lots of garden vegetables, as Will Allen points out. Growing your own vegetables makes eating them more fun and gives you exercise as well. Plus, gardening makes you very aware of how you're using the land around you and what you can do to help that land be its most productive.

Irish American Soda Bread

10–12 servings

Immigrant farmers grew the first wheat in our region. The farmers grew wheat to make breads and other baked goods for their families. They also earned money by selling their wheat crops. Immigrant farmers used wheat in their favorite baked goods, following traditional recipes from their homelands. Cornish newcomers made yellow-colored saffron rolls and caraway seed biscuits. Jewish immigrants made a rich egg bread called *challah* (pronounced **kah**-lah). People from Russia and Poland liked rye bread, and those from Norway made a flat bread (*flatbrød* in Norwegian) that baked up thin and crispy.

This is a recipe for Irish soda bread, another baked item made from wheat. Traditionally, soda bread is made with raisins. But for a modern Wisconsin version, you could use dried cherries from Door County. (If the cherries are larger than raisins, you can mix them with 1 teaspoon of flour and chop them up before you add them to the recipe.)

Directions:

1. Heat oven to 375 degrees. Grease a baking sheet, or line it with buttered parchment paper.

2. Combine flour, sugar, baking powder, baking soda, and salt in a large mixing bowl. Use a whisk to mix the ingredients very well.

3. Stir in the raisins or dried cherries.

4. In another bowl, mix egg, yogurt or buttermilk, and butter. Whisk until well combined.

Harvested wheat

Ingredients:

1⅔ cups whole-wheat pastry flour or
    regular white flour, plus more for
    dusting your hands
⅓ cup sugar
1⅛ teaspoons baking powder
½ teaspoon baking soda
½ teaspoon salt
1 cup raisins or dried tart cherries
1 large egg
¾ cup pourable plain yogurt or
    buttermilk

4 tablespoons butter, melted
Softened butter for spreading on bread
    (optional)
Jam for spreading on bread (optional)

You Will Need:

Baking sheet
Parchment paper (optional)
Butter to grease baking sheet or
    parchment paper
Large and medium mixing bowls
Measuring cups and spoons
Whisk
Wooden spoons
Toothpicks
Wire cooling rack

5. Add the egg mixture to the flour mixture. Stir the 2 mixtures until they are barely combined. The dough will be kind of sticky.

6. Scrape the dough onto the baking sheet. Dust your hands with flour and then form the dough into a mound that's about 7 inches wide. (Don't smooth the mound—it's supposed to be lumpy and bumpy looking.)

7. Bake the bread for 25–30 minutes. To tell when it's done, insert a toothpick near the center of the bread and then pull it out. If the toothpick looks clean, the bread is done. If it has sticky dough attached to it, bake a minute or 2 longer and then test it again.

8. Leave the bread on the pan while you let it cool on a rack. Serve the bread warm or at room temperature. You can slice it thickly or break it into large chunks to eat. (Add some butter and jam!)

Potato Pancakes

10–12 three-inch pancakes

At farmers' markets, you can find potatoes in many colors.

Wisconsin has always been a "potato state," partly because our climate and soil, especially in the central sand counties, make this a good place for potatoes to grow. Today Wisconsin is the number three potato producer in the nation. Potato farmers here grow lots of different kinds of potatoes, some with fun names like Goldrush, Ruby Crescent, and Russian Banana Fingerling!

You might think of pancakes as being made with flour, milk, and eggs and served for breakfast, but some are made with potatoes. Norwegian *lefse* are pancakes made from mashed potatoes. Germans made pancakes with grated potatoes and served them with applesauce and bratwurst. Jewish cooks added onions to their potato pancakes and called them *latkes* (**lot**-keez). Latkes are a traditional dish for Hanukkah (**hah**-nu-kuh), the Festival of Lights.

Tips for Grating Potatoes

Potatoes turn brown very quickly after they have been grated. Don't leave them standing too long! You can also put the grated potatoes in water while you do the rest of the grating. Then drain them well.

Directions:

1. Crack the eggs into a large bowl. Beat them with a whisk until smooth.

2. Peel the potatoes with a vegetable peeler. (Or you can scrub the potatoes with a vegetable brush and leave the skins on.)

3. Grate the potatoes on the large holes of a grater. Watch your fingers! As soon as you are done grating the potatoes, place them on cloth or paper towels. Fold up the towels around the potatoes and squeeze out as much liquid as you can from them.

Ingredients:

2 eggs

1¼ pounds (about 4 medium-sized) baking potatoes

⅓ cup flour

1 teaspoon salt

¼ teaspoon baking powder

¼ teaspoon black pepper

Vegetable oil for frying the pancakes

Applesauce and sour cream, or maple syrup

You Will Need:

Large bowl

Whisk

Vegetable peeler

Vegetable brush (optional)

Cloth or paper towels

Grater ⟶

Measuring cups and spoons

Wooden spoons

Large, heavy skillet (a cast-iron one works best)

Scoop

Metal spatula

4. Add the squeezed potatoes to the eggs. Stir in the flour, salt, baking powder, and pepper.

5. Heat a large, heavy skillet over medium heat for 3–4 minutes.

6. Slowly and carefully, add oil to the skillet; the oil should be ⅛ inch deep, so that it covers the bottom of the pan in a thin layer. Let the oil heat a minute or 2; it should be hot enough to make the potato mixture sizzle when you add it. Be careful!

7. Add a scoop of pancake mixture to the hot oil and flatten it with a spoon. Continue with more scoops of the mixture until the pan is filled but not crowded. Turn the pancakes over, one at a time, with a spatula. Cook pancakes until they are golden brown on both sides, about 4 minutes on each side.

8. Lift out the pancakes with the spatula and drain them on paper towels. Make more batches until all the batter is used up. Serve the pancakes with applesauce or syrup. Sour cream also goes nicely with the applesauce.

Cheesy Smashed Potatoes with Toasted Nuts

6–8 servings

The potato was a very important vegetable for Wisconsin's early settlers. During our long, cold winters, potatoes were easy to store in cellars or basements. Sometimes, when meat and other vegetables were scarce or hard to get, families ate potatoes three times a day. They fixed potatoes many different ways: mashed, fried, baked, roasted, and boiled, and in pancakes, soups, salad, bread, and dumplings.

Today we don't eat potatoes as often as the settlers did, but cooks still come up with interesting ways to prepare them. The idea for this recipe came from a Wisconsin chef, Eric Rupert. Eric uses many local ingredients in his dishes. In this one he combines potatoes with cheese and wild hickory nuts. Can you think of other local ingredients to add to potatoes?

Directions:

1. Heat oven to 325 degrees. Spread out nuts on a baking pan.

2. Bake nuts for about 10 minutes until they are lightly toasted and smell good, stirring them once or twice while they are cooking so that they don't burn. Let the nuts cool off while you cook the potatoes.

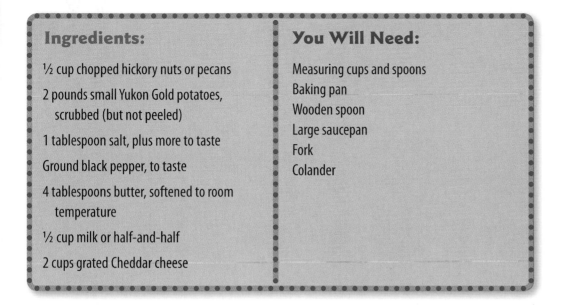

Ingredients:

½ cup chopped hickory nuts or pecans

2 pounds small Yukon Gold potatoes, scrubbed (but not peeled)

1 tablespoon salt, plus more to taste

Ground black pepper, to taste

4 tablespoons butter, softened to room temperature

½ cup milk or half-and-half

2 cups grated Cheddar cheese

You Will Need:

Measuring cups and spoons
Baking pan
Wooden spoon
Large saucepan
Fork
Colander

3. Place potatoes and a tablespoon of salt in a large saucepan of water. Bring the water to a boil. Cook the potatoes until they are tender when you poke them with a fork, 12–15 minutes.

4. Drain the potatoes in a colander. Return the potatoes to the pot. Place the pot over low heat on the stove for a minute or 2 (this will dry off the rest of the water from the potatoes). Stir gently to keep the potatoes from sticking. Remove from heat.

5. Add butter, milk (or half-and-half), and some salt and pepper to the potatoes. Use a large fork to smash everything together. Add the cheese and nuts and smash the potatoes a little more. Then dig in and enjoy!

Seven-Layer Pea Salad

8 servings

Peas were one of the earliest large-production crops in Wisconsin. As you read on page 67, we can thank Albert Landreth for that. In the late 1880s, Mr. Landreth's pea-canning factory in Manitowoc had a major impact on commercial agriculture in our state.

Seven-Layer Pea Salad is a traditional dish that is often served at potlucks and picnics. Today, most people make it with fresh or frozen peas, not canned peas. (Sorry, Mr. Landreth!)

A large clear-glass bowl is the perfect container for this salad. It will show off all the layers in a colorful way. For an extra touch, place 3 tablespoons of the peas and 2 tablespoons of the cheese in a small bowl before you make the salad. Then sprinkle these on top of the finished salad before you serve it.

Governor Phil La Follette looked pleased at a display promoting Wisconsin's pea crop in 1938.

Ingredients:

3 cups thinly sliced spinach leaves

1 cup diced green or red bell peppers

½ cup thinly sliced green onions

1 bag (10 ounces) frozen peas, thawed and drained on paper towels

1½ cups shredded Cheddar cheese

1 cup finely diced ham

1 cup mayonnaise to spread over the top of the salad

You Will Need:

Knife

Cutting board

Colander

Measuring cups

Paper towels

Large glass bowl or 9-by-13-inch glass baking dish

Small bowl (optional)

Directions:

1. Prepare the ingredients as described in the list above.

2. Layer the ingredients in the bowl or baking dish in the order in which they are listed above.

3. Chill the salad in the refrigerator for 2 or more hours.

4. Bring the salad to the table so all the diners can see the layers through the glass. Then toss the salad and serve it up.

CSA Veggies and Dip

1¼ cups dip

Imagine getting a treasure box every week. That's what joining a CSA farm is like. In this chapter you've learned that CSA stands for *community-supported agriculture*. Members of a CSA buy part of a farmer's harvest and get it delivered to their neighborhood every week. Being part of CSA is a great way for growers and eaters to know and support each other. And what happens when all those fresh, fun vegetable "treasures" find their way into the kitchen? Exciting things—including this platter of colorful veggies with a cheesy, herby dip.

Directions:

1. Pull the leaves off the herb sprigs. Put the leaves into a food processor or blender. Add the cottage cheese, cream cheese, lemon juice, and chopped green onion. Sprinkle in a little black pepper. Blend the mixture until it is pretty smooth (it doesn't have to be perfectly smooth).

2. Scrape the dip into a medium bowl. Place the bowl in the middle of a big round platter. Arrange all the vegetables in little piles around the dip. Cover dip and vegetables with plastic wrap and chill until ready to serve.

Caution

This recipe calls for the use of a food processor, which has very sharp blades. Be sure an adult is present and watching closely when you are handling the food processor.

Ingredients:

1 fistful of fresh dill, mint, or cilantro sprigs (or use some of each)

1 cup cottage cheese

¼ cup cream cheese

Juice of ½ lemon

1 green onion, chopped into 1-inch pieces

Ground black pepper

Raw vegetables (choose several from the following list or think of other vegetables that you like):

Asparagus spears

Peeled baby carrots

Sugar snap peas

Kohlrabi, sliced thin

Baby zucchini, cut lengthwise into wedges

Radishes

Cherry tomatoes

You Will Need:

Measuring cups and spoons

Food processor or blender

Rubber spatula

Medium bowl

Sharp knife

Cutting board

Large, round platter

Plastic wrap

CHAPTER 4

Flavors from Meat and Dairy Farms

EVER SINCE EARLY INDIANS hunted mammoths and mastodons as the glaciers melted, people in Wisconsin have enjoyed eating meat. Fast-forward to the 1800s, when butchers around the state cut steaks, roasts, chops, and stew meat and ground meat to make these products easy to buy locally for people who lived in towns and cities. Most Wisconsin farmers did their own butchering during that period. Wisconsin farmers today have helped make the state one of the top 10 in the country for sales of livestock products: meat from beef cattle, hogs, and other animals, such as bison or lamb.

But if you ask Americans the first word they think of when someone says "Wisconsin," the answer will probably be "cheese." In this chapter, you'll find out just why we're known as cheeseheads and why our grill-outs and tailgate parties almost always include brats.

There are six different breeds of dairy cow—Ayrshire, Brown Swiss, Guernsey, Holstein, Jersey, and Milking Shorthorn—and all are found on Wisconsin dairy farms.

Got Milk! And Butter! And Cream!

People from Wisconsin were not always known as cheeseheads! In fact, the black-and-white Holstein dairy cow began to be an important part of the state's agriculture only after wheat failed as a crop in the late 1800s. Partly that's because dairy cows demand more attention than wheat. Once it is planted, wheat grows by itself until harvest time, but cows must be milked every day, sometimes more than once a day. But this wasn't the only reason that dairying took a while to catch on in Wisconsin.

Pioneer farmers produced only enough milk and vegetables to feed their own families. But to earn money from milk—money to buy clothes, furniture, and other necessities—farmers had to make many changes. They had to produce good milk, and more of it. They also had to be able to sell their milk year-round. So farmers needed more cows, and they needed to feed their cows over the long winters. They also needed to build large, solid barns to keep their cows warm and safe all winter long.

Before dairy farming became a big business in Wisconsin, most farmers kept just a cow or two to provide milk and cheese for their own family.

Here's a Wisconsin Holstein—a statue, that is—in Neillsville. Although Chatty Belle no longer talks, she used to tell visitors lots of facts about Wisconsin's dairy cows if you put a quarter in her slot!

But how could farmers store plenty of feed and keep it from spoiling? The problem was solved with the invention of silage, a fermented mixture of animal feed that could be stored and fed to cows during the winter. By the 1880s, farmers around the country, including a few in Wisconsin, were beginning to store silage in silos. Soon there were cylinder-shaped towers in farmyards all around the state.

Next, dairy farmers had to learn how to produce large quantities of dairy products that people would be willing to pay for. Dairy farm families were used to milking cows and making butter for themselves. Selling larger amounts of dairy products to others was another matter. In order to sell dairy products, such as butter and cheese, farmers had to make sure that the quality was high. That quality had to remain high each time the product was sold, or the customer would be disappointed.

High-quality milk tastes good and contains nutrients and plenty of butterfat. The dairy industry needed a way to distinguish low-quality milk from high-quality milk. Professor Stephen Babcock at the University of Wisconsin went to work on this problem. He decided to invent a test that would measure the amount of butterfat in milk. He wanted the test to be simple enough that it could be used by every dairy in the state.

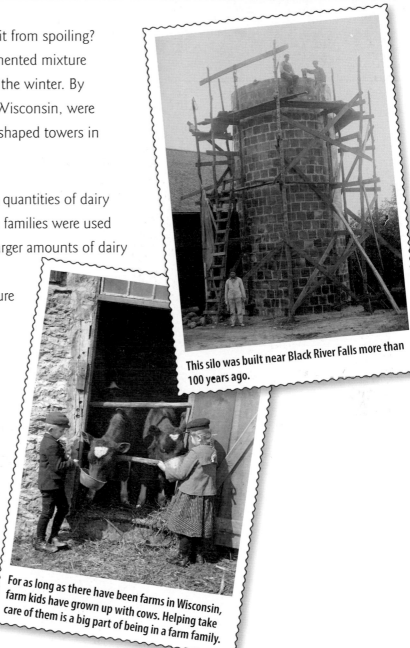

This silo was built near Black River Falls more than 100 years ago.

For as long as there have been farms in Wisconsin, farm kids have grown up with cows. Helping take care of them is a big part of being in a farm family.

Stephen Babcock with his butterfat tester

In 1890, Professor Babcock invented what became known as the Babcock test. Now that butterfat could be measured, the dairy industry could set rules for milk quality. Milk that was high quality was either bottled for drinking or made into cheese. Wisconsin dairies produced such high-quality butter that the state led the nation in butter making as early as 1909. In the early 2000s, Wisconsin was still producing about one-fourth of the nation's butter. It's easy to see that Stephen Babcock's invention improved the dairy industry in Wisconsin and throughout the United States.

Dairying reshaped the landscape of Wisconsin even more than wheat had. Cattle and feed crops—corn, oats, hay, and other grains that cows eat—replaced wheat fields. Farmers learned about new developments in farming by working with county extension agents (people who learn about the land and help people like farmers by sharing what they know) and by reading magazines like *Hoard's Dairyman*.

In 1942, Phyllis Paulson of Stoughton posed with the calf she planned to enter in the Junior Fair competition at the Wisconsin State Fair.

William Hoard and Hoard's Dairyman

Like many people with an interest in farming, William Dempster Hoard moved from New York to Wisconsin in the mid-1800s. He had already seen dairy farms replace wheat farming in New York, and he wanted to help Wisconsin farmers begin a real dairy industry here. So William Hoard wrote newspaper articles about good dairy farming practices in his Fort Atkinson newspaper, *The Jefferson County Union*. Then, in 1885, he began publishing *Hoard's Dairyman*, a magazine with plenty of information to help dairy farmers.

Hoard also started his own farm, so that every day he could practice the ideas he was sharing with others. *Hoard's Dairyman* is still going strong—over 120 years later! You can visit the Hoard home, now the Hoard Museum and National Dairy Shrine, in Fort Atkinson.

Wisconsin artist James Baird worked for *Hoard's Dairyman* for more than 40 years. He created many beautiful paintings that appeared on the cover of the annual Christmas issue, including this one from 1995. Can you see the star on top of the silo?

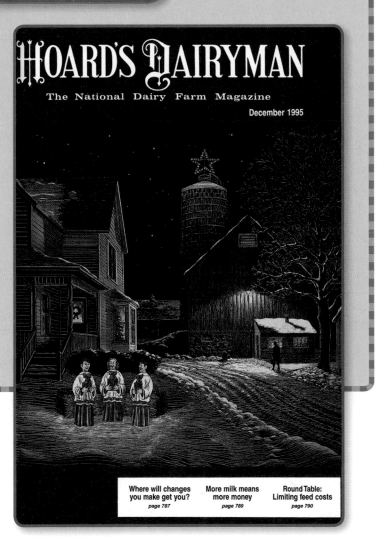

HOARD'S DAIRYMAN

The National Dairy Farm Magazine

December 1995

| Where will changes you make get you? page 787 | More milk means more money page 789 | Round Table: Limiting feed costs page 790 |

Say Cheese!

Many of the first dairy farmers and cheese makers in Wisconsin came from New York and from Switzerland, Germany, and other places in Europe where dairying was a tradition. They had already learned that not all kinds of cows are suited to dairy. They knew that some cows, such as the Holsteins, produced more milk than others. Some of these immigrant farmers had also learned to make cheese before they came to this country.

Cheese maker Casper Jaggi and other workers in the cooling room at the Coldren Swiss cheese factory in Brodhead in the early 1900s

Today, dairy farming and cheese making take place in almost every part of Wisconsin. Cheddar cheese may be our number one variety, but brick and Colby cheese were both invented here. Swiss immigrants who settled in south-central Wisconsin made Monroe the Swiss and Limburger cheese capital of the state. Limburger is famous for its strong aroma and rich flavor, and Monroe is famous for being the town where all of the country's Limburger comes from!

By 1978, the state's cheese factories produced more than a third of the cheese made in the United States. As people from more places settled in Wisconsin, our cheese factories began producing cheese to meet their tastes: mozzarella for pizza and Mexican cheese varieties for enchiladas and quesadillas, for example. In recent years interest in cheese has grown a great deal. Now Wisconsin cheese makers produce hundreds of varieties of cheese to meet the demand.

In 2010, more than 90 percent of the state's milk was used in cheese making, and people all over the world were buying Wisconsin's cheese.

This 1937 dairy industry promotion shows Wisconsin as a table where cheese and butter are being served.

A huge wheel of Swiss cheese is all ready to go at the Edelweiss Creamery in Monroe. Wouldn't you like to take a bite?

Changes in Dairyland

As with other kinds of farming, dairying has its own problems that affect farm families. From the 1930s on, the amount of milk that farms produced grew while the number of farms fell. How did that happen? Technology played a large role. Mechanized equipment affected the way farmers farmed and the way their cows were milked. Fewer farmers with larger farms were able to grow more food on less land.

And this was happening not just in Wisconsin. By 1996, huge factory farms in California had helped make it the nation's largest milk-producing state. Although the number of dairy farms in Wisconsin was still decreasing in the early 2000s, our dairy industry had already begun to grow in a new direction.

The Hemstead farm is one of hundreds of farms that produce milk for Organic Valley in La Farge, Wisconsin. Organic Valley is the nation's largest farm cooperative. A cooperative, or co-op, is a company that markets and sells the products from many farms.

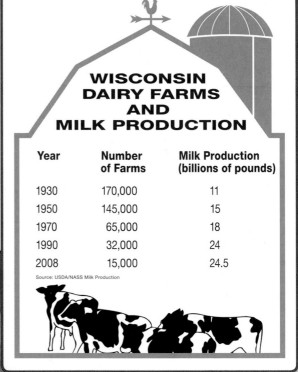

WISCONSIN DAIRY FARMS AND MILK PRODUCTION

Year	Number of Farms	Milk Production (billions of pounds)
1930	170,000	11
1950	145,000	15
1970	65,000	18
1990	32,000	24
2008	15,000	24.5

Source: USDA/NASS Milk Production

Take a look at the numbers on this chart. It shows that the amount of milk produced on Wisconsin farms has increased, but the number of farms has decreased. How did that happen? Mechanized farm equipment made it possible to milk a lot of cows at one time. Farms and herds have gotten bigger, but the total number of farms has shrunk.

We have become leaders in organic dairy farming. You learned in chapter 3 that organic farming means farming without the use of human-made chemicals such as fertilizers and weed killers. Organic dairy farmers allow their cows to graze in open pastures as much of the year as possible. These farmers also do not give their cows any chemicals that can make them produce more milk. Many people believe that not only is organic milk better for you, but it also *tastes* better. Even though organic dairying is just a tiny part of the overall dairy industry in Wisconsin, it is growing. And that's a very good sign.

Another part of Wisconsin's dairy industry that is growing is specialty cheese—that means cheese made in small batches, sometimes even by hand. When Wisconsin first became a dairy state, about 150 years ago, all the cheese makers worked in small batches, of course. But for the past 30 years, most of the cheese made in Wisconsin was big batches of Cheddar and mozzarella, made in large factories to be shipped all over the country.

However, specialty cheese is becoming popular again. Many small dairy farmers who could not compete with huge factory farms have started making cheese from their own cows' (or goats' or sheep's) milk to earn more money and stay in business. And many of the cheese makers who produce these cheeses use recipes and methods from a long time ago. Others start with an old style of cheese and add new flavors for a twist.

Today Wisconsin is a leader in the specialty cheese business. In fact, Wisconsin cheese makers now produce half of the specialty cheese made in the entire United States. And Wisconsin's specialty cheeses win more national and international awards than cheese from any other state.

Cheese lovers everywhere are excited about the new specialty cheese flavors coming from Wisconsin.

Wisconsin cheese maker Marieke Penterman is proud of the Gouda cheese she makes at Hollands Family Farm in Thorp.

Meat Eaters' Heaven

Sausage is one of Wisconsin's most beloved forms of meat. Wisconsinites especially love bratwurst, better known as brats, the sausage that you find being grilled at every kind of celebration—from backyard cookouts to athletic events and county fairs. Madison's "World's Largest Brat Fest" takes place on Memorial Day weekend each year and draws a large audience of brat lovers to raise money for local charities. Visitors to the festival eat more than 200,000 brats during this four-day event!

The annual Taste of Madison festival just *has* to offer a brat fry, since brats seem to be part of most celebrations in Wisconsin.

Ever wonder *why* folks in Wisconsin love brats and other kinds of sausage? In the 1800s, immigrants from sausage-making and sausage-eating countries in central Europe—like Germany, Bohemia (now the Czech Republic), and Poland—headed to Wisconsin. Small and large meat processors all over the state make sausage, though Sheboygan considers itself the state's brat capital.

Sausage making involves grinding many parts of animal scraps and mixing them with different kinds of seasonings. Indians in Wisconsin originally made a kind of sausage (called pemmican) from dried meat, corn, wild rice, and berries. Non-Indians have created sausage according to their own home countries' traditions. Now we are fortunate to be able to enjoy brats and the many other kinds of sausage, from Polish to Italian and Mexican, found in grocery stores and butcher shops across the state.

These butchers were ready to help their customer at a meat market in Palmyra about 100 years ago.

The Milwaukee Brewers' Famous Racing Sausages

Baseball may not always be in season, but the Brewers' Racing Sausages are always a favorite Wisconsin tradition! The five sausages—#1 (German bratwurst); #2 (Polish sausage); #3 (Italian sausage); #4 (hot dog); and #5 (Mexican chorizo)—are officially known as the Klement's Famous Racing Sausages. Klement's sausages are the brand served at Miller Park.

The Racing Sausages first appeared at the games as a cartoon on the scoreboard. Then in May 1994, the first live sausage race took place, with the first three sausages participating. The hot dog joined the others soon after, and the chorizo was added in 2006. At first they raced only on Sunday afternoons to entertain the family audience. But the sausages were so popular that they began racing during every game and appearing at other events as well.

Which is your favorite Racing Sausage?

Along with the sausage varieties that came to Wisconsin with folks from central Europe, other meat dishes immigrated here as well. The Cornish lead miners and their families who immigrated to Mineral Point in the 1820s and 1830s brought their tradition of making meat turnovers with them. Workingmen could easily pack these pasties in their lunch pails. Scandinavians made their beloved meatballs in gravy, and Germans cooked up dishes like pork hocks and sauerkraut. Then the 20th century brought so many new people to Wisconsin that our foodways grew in new directions, including Mexican fajitas made from skirt steak, Southeast Asian appetizers using ground meat, Indian meat curries, and Middle Eastern lamb kabobs.

These women made sausages at the Oscar Mayer company in the mid-1900s.

Homemade Butter

¾–1 cup butter

Churning butter by hand was hard work. It was done mostly by the mothers and daughters of the farm family.

Butter is cream that has been whipped so much that the cream separates into two parts. One part is liquid, called buttermilk, and the other is a soft solid—and that's called butter!

Most butter today is whipped in large machines at creameries (butter factories). But long ago many pioneer farmers kept a cow on their farms so that they could have milk, cheese, and butter to eat with their meals. Pioneer women made butter "by hand." But that doesn't mean they made butter *in* their hands. They used a butter churn.

A butter churn is a wooden container with a special stick that has paddles on the end of it. A member of the farm family—usually the mother or an older daughter—put the cream in the wooden container and then used the paddle stick to whip, or churn, the cream until it turned to butter. It took strength and patience to make butter—it took a lot of churning and a lot of time. But good, fresh butter was worth it! The whole family enjoyed butter.

Here is a way to make butter "by hand" today. Instead of a butter churn or a large machine, you can use electric beaters. The best cream to use for this recipe is organic heavy cream. Organic cream will make a pure-tasting butter—it will taste the way butter did in pioneer days.

Directions:

1. Pour the cream into a deep bowl and whip it using a handheld electric mixer. Carefully move the beaters up and down and all through the cream as you are whipping. It will be several minutes before the cream begins to turn to butter. At first, it will look like a creamy liquid. Then after a couple of minutes the cream will begin to thicken. Next, it will form soft mounds, and after that it will form into stiff peaks. Keep whipping, because now is when little bits of butter will begin to form. You'll also see a milky-looking liquid—that is the buttermilk that the butter is throwing off. Keep going until larger blobs of butter appear and begin to stick together. Eventually the butter blob will no longer throw off any more liquid.

2. Drain off the liquid into a bowl or glass. You can drink this buttermilk or add it to a recipe such as mashed potatoes or a cream soup.

3. Now rinse the butter in the bowl with cold water, drain it, and squeeze out more liquid with your hands.

4. Pat the butter with paper towels to dry it off. Some people add a little salt at this point and work it into the butter. But that isn't necessary.

5. Spread it on some bread and enjoy real homemade butter!

6. To store the butter, wrap it up well and keep it in the refrigerator.

Ingredients:

1 pint organic heavy cream, at room temperature

Salt (optional)

You Will Need:

Handheld electric mixer
Deep bowl
Paper towels

Cream Puffs

12 cream puffs

Cream puffs have been a favorite Wisconsin State Fair food for many years. With their cream filling and powdered sugar topping, they are messy to eat but oh, so good!

Have you ever eaten a cream puff? It's a kind of dessert "sandwich." It is made by splitting a special pastry puff in half, filling it with whipped cream, and topping it with powdered sugar.

One of the best places to get a cream puff in Wisconsin is at the State Fair, which takes place every summer at State Fair Park in West Allis, near Milwaukee. Cream puffs are one of many special Wisconsin dairy foods served at the fair—and they are probably most people's favorite, too! Members of the Wisconsin Bakers Association bake large pastries, fill them with mounds of real whipped cream, and sell them at the fair. Cream puffs became popular at the State Fair in the 1940s, during World War II. Cream was in short supply then, so visitors to the fair would line up by the hundreds to get a cream puff.

State Fair visitors still line up for cream puffs. Nowadays the Wisconsin Bakers Association serves more than 50,000 cream puffs each day at the State Fair!

Directions:

1. Heat oven to 450 degrees. Grease a large baking sheet or line it with parchment paper.

2. Place water, butter, and salt in a heavy saucepan over medium-low heat. Bring the mixture to a boil and then give it a brief stir.

3. Using a wooden spoon, quickly but carefully stir in all the sifted flour at once, until everything is well combined. Keep stirring the mixture over the heat until it forms a ball and no longer clings to the sides of the pan. Then remove the pan from the heat and let it stand to cool for 3–4 minutes.

4. Use a wooden spoon to beat I of the eggs into the mixture in the pan. Beat it in very well. Repeat this with each of the remaining 3 eggs. Be sure to beat well after you add each egg. The dough should be stiff but smooth.

5. Using a ¼-cup scoop or large spoon, scoop out the batter and place the scoopfuls 2–3 inches apart on the greased baking sheet, making as many rows as will fit on the sheet. Bake for 10 minutes.

6. Reduce the oven temperature to 350 degrees and bake about 25 minutes more. (If your stove has a window, it's fun to watch the dough rise and turn into the puffs.) The puffs are done when they turn golden brown and feel firm when you touch them.

7. Turn off the oven. Pull out the puffs and gently poke each one *once* with a toothpick. Now put the puffs back into the oven. Leave the oven door open and let the puffs cool off inside. (Poking the puffs and cooling them slowly also help prevent soggy puffs.)

8. When the puffs are completely cool, you should store them in an airtight container. To serve the cream puffs, cut them in half from side to side. Fill each bottom half with whipped cream. Place the tops on the puffs. Use a sifter to sprinkle powdered sugar over the whole puff. Dig in. Aren't cream puffs wonderful?

Ingredients:

1 cup water

8 tablespoons butter, cut into chunks

¼ teaspoon salt

1 cup flour, sifted

4 eggs, at room temperature

Real Whipped Cream (see page 110)

Powdered sugar for sprinkling over the cream puffs

You Will Need:

Large baking sheet, with butter for greasing

Parchment paper (optional)

Measuring cups and spoons

Heavy saucepan

Wooden spoons

Scoop or large spoon

Toothpicks

Sifter

Real Whipped Cream

6–8 cups whipped cream

Real whipped cream is a special treat. It doesn't take very long to make, especially with an electric mixer. Imagine if you lived on a farm long ago and didn't have electricity. You'd have to use a whisk and whip the cream by hand. Your arm would get tired, but it would be worth it!

Ingredients:

1 pint heavy cream

½ teaspoon vanilla extract

2–3 tablespoons sugar (you can use granulated or powdered sugar)

You Will Need:

Deep bowl (stainless steel or copper; do not use plastic)
Electric mixer (handheld or stand)
Measuring spoons

Directions:

1. Place the heavy cream in a deep, chilled bowl.

2. Use an electric mixer to beat the cream until it begins to form soft mounds.

3. Beat in the vanilla.

4. Keep beating while you sprinkle in the sugar a little at a time. (If you're using a handheld mixer, it helps to have 2 people working on this together—1 to beat and 1 to sprinkle in the sugar.)

5. Stop beating when firm peaks form. Voilà! Real whipped cream.

Tips for Whipping Cream

• Use heavy cream or whipping cream. Avoid cream that is labeled "ultrapasteurized"—it won't whip very well.

• Use a stainless steel or copper bowl (not plastic). Chill the bowl and the mixer beaters before you start.

• If you're using a hand mixer, move the beaters up, down, and around the cream as you beat it.

• Don't add the vanilla extract and sugar until after the cream begins to take shape.

• Don't overbeat the cream (or it will turn to butter!). Stop beating as soon as the cream forms firm peaks.

Wisconsin Cheese and Sausage Platter

Any number of servings

Wisconsin is world-famous for its cheese. The state is also well-known for sausage. So it makes sense that a platter of cheese and sausage is a popular appetizer in Wisconsin. Cheese and sausage platters are served at parties, picnics, and many other kinds of gatherings. Does your family ever serve them?

Wisconsin has a state bird (robin), a state drink (milk), and a state flower (wood violet). What if Wisconsin also had a state appetizer? Maybe it would be a cheese and sausage platter!

Directions:

1. Arrange the cheese and sausage on a platter. You can put them in separate piles. Or you can line them up in rows, or make another kind of arrangement. Add some cherry tomatoes and parsley sprigs to decorate the platter. If you aren't going to serve the platter right away, wrap it in plastic wrap and keep it refrigerated until serving time.

2. Place the crackers in a basket and serve them with the cheese and sausage platter.

Ingredients:

Sliced Colby or Cheddar cheese

Sliced Monterey Jack or Co-Jack cheese

Sliced Swiss cheese

Fresh, squeaky cheese curds

Sliced summer sausage

Garnishes: Cherry tomatoes and parsley sprigs

Assorted crackers

You Will Need:

Platter
Plastic wrap
Serving basket

Quesadillas

Any number of servings

Most Wisconsin kids grow up eating grilled-cheese sandwiches. Think of these Mexican-style quesadillas as another type of grilled cheese.

Ingredients:

Whole-wheat flour tortillas or corn tortillas

Softened butter

Grated or thinly sliced cheese (Cheddar, Muenster, Swiss, or your favorite)

Chopped green onions (optional)

Bottled salsa (optional)

You Will Need:

Cast-iron or other heavy skillet

Butter knife

Metal or sturdy heat-resistant plastic spatula

Cutting board

Sharp knife

Directions:

1. Heat a cast-iron or other heavy skillet over medium heat for 5 minutes. (If you're using a nonstick skillet, heat it for only 2 minutes.)

2. Make the quesadillas one at a time: Butter 2 tortillas, each on 1 side only. Place 1 of the buttered tortillas in the hot pan, with the buttered side down. Spread cheese over the tortilla. Sprinkle on some green onions, if you like them. Put the second tortilla on top, with the buttered side facing up this time.

3. Cook the quesadilla until it is browned on the bottom. You can lift it up with a spatula to check underneath.

4. Work the spatula all the way under the quesadilla. Then flip the quesadilla over to cook the other side. Let it cook until the cheese looks melted and the bottom is browned.

5. Move the quesadilla to a cutting board and cut it in half or in quarters.

6. You can also make a quesadilla with 1 tortilla: Butter 1 side of the tortilla, and put some cheese in the middle of the unbuttered side. Fold the tortilla over to make a half-moon shape. Then cook the half-moon on both sides. Serve the quesadillas with salsa.

Easy Tomato Feta Sauce (for Pasta, Rice, or Couscous)

6–8 servings

Not all of Wisconsin's cheeses are made in large cheese factories. Some cheese makers today craft their cheese in small batches using traditional methods, sometimes by hand instead of using machines. These cheeses are called specialty or artisanal cheeses. And not all of the cheese is made from cow's milk. Some cheese makers use goat's or sheep's milk to make their cheese. Feta is a specialty cheese that can be made from cow's milk, goat's milk, or sheep's milk. Feta is a crumbly, white, salty-tasting cheese. It originally came from Greece.

Directions:

1. Use a serrated knife to slice the cherry tomatoes in half. Place the tomatoes, feta, olive oil, dill, and vinegar in a large bowl. Stir to combine.

2. Let the sauce you just made stand for 10–20 minutes, stirring it occasionally. (Letting the sauce stand and stirring it once in a while will make it taste better. It's as if the ingredients are getting to know each other a little better.)

3. While the sauce ingredients are getting to know each other, cook some pasta, rice, or couscous. Follow the directions on the package.

4. Now back to the sauce. Add salt and pepper to taste.

5. When the pasta, rice, or couscous is done, add the sauce and toss everything together. Or you can serve the sauce on top of the pasta, rice, or couscous.

Ingredients:

2 pints ripe cherry tomatoes

1 cup crumbled feta cheese

4–5 tablespoons olive oil

3–4 tablespoons chopped fresh dill

2 tablespoons balsamic vinegar

Cooked pasta, rice, or couscous*

Salt and freshly ground black pepper

You Will Need:

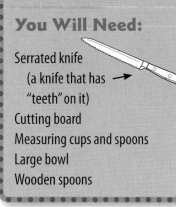

Serrated knife (a knife that has "teeth" on it)

Cutting board

Measuring cups and spoons

Large bowl

Wooden spoons

* Couscous is made from wheat. Think of it as tiny little grains of pasta.

Sausage Potato Cakes

4–6 servings

Butchering was a very important task for immigrant farmers of the 19th century. After an animal was butchered, the whole family helped in preparing the meat to preserve it for future meals. They smoked some of the meat over a wood fire to make ham or bacon. Some of the meat was dried in the sun. And some of the meat was made into sausages—lots of sausages!

Each family had its own traditional recipes for making sausage. The recipes came from the old countries. For example, Slovaks (people from Slovakia) made sausage with rice. Norwegians favored *rull*, which is strips of pork and beef with chopped onions and seasoning, all rolled up inside a large, flat piece of beef or veal. Germans made sausages with oats, eggs, or apples in them.

Here is a simple Swedish recipe for mashed potatoes mixed with pork sausage. This was a supper dish, but it can be eaten for lunch or breakfast, too.

Rows of sausages were a tempting treat for these hungry window shoppers in Milwaukee in 1967.

<table>
<tr><td>

Ingredients:

2 eggs

½ pound bulk pork sausage

3 cups cold mashed potatoes

Salt and black pepper

Cooking oil or butter for frying the cakes

</td><td>

You Will Need:

Small and large bowls

Cast-iron or other heavy skillet

Spatula

Slotted spoon

Measuring cup

</td></tr>
</table>

Directions:

1. Beat the eggs in a small bowl. Set them aside.

2. Heat a cast-iron or other heavy skillet over medium-high heat. When the skillet is hot, add the sausage. Use a spatula to break up and crumble the sausage as it cooks. Cook the sausage until it browns, with no pink showing in the meat.

3. Use a slotted spoon to move the cooked sausage to a bowl. Add the potatoes and beaten eggs to the sausage. Sprinkle with salt and pepper to taste. You can also add a little of the fat that's left in the pan, if you like.

4. Mix everything together and then, using clean hands, form the mixture into patties. A good way to do this is to roll the mixture into balls, then flatten and shape the balls into patties.

5. Place a clean skillet over medium heat. Add some oil or butter—just enough to coat the bottom of the pan.

6. Add the patties to the pan (but don't crowd them together). Brown them on both sides. Serve hot.

Bratwurst Vegetable Soup

6–8 servings

You've probably eaten bratwurst before, but have you ever eaten bratwurst in a soup? Today most people eat brats that have been grilled and then placed in a bun with mustard or sauerkraut (and maybe some onions). But in days gone by, bratwurst was a sausage that people ate with a knife and fork. If any sausage was left over, it might have gone into a soup like this one.

Buttered rye bread and a glass of apple cider go really well with this soup.

Directions:

1. Heat the butter in a soup pot over medium heat.

2. Stir in the onions, carrots, celery, and fennel seeds. Cook the vegetables for 5 minutes, stirring often.

3. Stir in the sliced bratwurst, beef broth, water, potatoes, corn, pickles, and dill weed. Bring the mixture to a simmer. Cover the pot. Adjust the heat so that the soup will slowly simmer. Let it simmer 40 minutes.

4. Add salt and pepper to your liking. You can eat the soup now. Or, to let it develop more flavor, turn off the heat and let the soup cool for an hour or more. Reheat the soup and serve it up.

Ingredients:

1 tablespoon butter

1 cup chopped onions

1 cup thinly sliced carrots

½ cup thinly sliced celery

2 teaspoons fennel seeds

2 cooked bratwursts, sliced thin

3 cans (14½ ounces each) beef broth

1 cup water

1 cup thinly sliced potatoes

½ cup corn kernels

⅓ cup thinly sliced dill pickles

½ teaspoon dried dill weed

Salt and black pepper

You Will Need:

Sharp knife for slicing

Cutting board

Measuring cups and spoons

Soup pot

Wooden spoon

This Wisconsin girl stirred up a big pot of something yummy in the 1930s. Do you think it was Bratwurst Vegetable Soup?

Larb

12 servings

Hmong families who came to Wisconsin from Laos, Vietnam, and Thailand make a ground beef dish called *larb*. The ground beef is cooked, mixed with spices, and then cooled to room temperature. Then the meat is rolled up in lettuce leaves with fresh vegetables and herbs, to be eaten with your hands. Hmong Americans add a spicy dressing to the roll-ups, too. Larb is a salad that you can eat without a fork!

Hmong families enjoy larb made with other kinds of meat, too—chicken, pork, venison, duck, and turkey. Sometimes they make it with raw fish.

Serve these Laotian roll-ups with cooked white rice (but you'll need a fork for that).

Directions:

1. Place meat in a large pot. Add enough water to just barely cover the meat. Bring the water to a simmer. Cook the meat, uncovered, at a low simmer until all the pink is gone, breaking it up with a spoon as it cooks.

2. Use a colander to drain the water off the meat. Let the meat cool.

3. Place the rice cereal grains in a skillet. Put the skillet on the stove and turn the heat on to medium. Cook the rice grains for a few minutes, until they are lightly browned. Be sure to stir often while they are heating. Turn the heat off and let the grains cool.

Ingredients:

3 pounds ground round beef

⅓ cup uncooked cream of rice cereal

1 cup thinly sliced green onions

1 cup finely chopped fresh mint

Juice of 4 limes or 2 lemons

2 tablespoons chopped cilantro

2 teaspoons salt

½ teaspoon red pepper flakes (or more, if you like hot, spicy food)

24 or more large Bibb lettuce leaves (or another kind of soft leaf lettuce)

Additional vegetables and herbs (use any or all of them):

Sliced green cabbage

Chopped green onions

Diced cucumbers

Fresh mint leaves

Fresh basil leaves

Sliced radishes

Asian chili sauce (bottled)

You Will Need:

Measuring cups and spoons

Large pot

Wooden spoon

Colander

Skillet

Large bowl and several small bowls

Sharp knife

Cutting board

Serving spoons

4. Put the ground meat and rice grains into a large bowl and add the green onions, chopped mint, lime or lemon juice, cilantro, salt, and red pepper flakes. Mix well, and form the mixture into a big mound in the bowl.

5. Prepare the additional vegetables and herbs that you chose. Put them in separate bowls.

6. To serve, put all the bowls on the table. Each person eating makes his or her own roll-ups. To make a roll-up: Place a piece of lettuce on a plate. Add some of the meat mixture and whatever additional vegetables and herbs you like. Add a little of the Asian chili sauce, too, if you like spicy food. Then fold the left and right sides of the lettuce leaf over the fillings. Now just roll it up and eat it.

Black-Eyed Peas with Ham Hocks

8 servings

Pleasant Ridge was a close community of African Americans in southwestern Wisconsin more than 100 years ago.

Pleasant Ridge is the name of an early black farming settlement in Wisconsin (see page 156). It was founded in 1848 by freed slaves from the South. In Wisconsin they raised farm animals and tended vegetable gardens. And they cooked Southern dishes like cornbread, fried chicken, and beans with ham hocks.

Many African American farm cooks were very skilled at using every part of an animal in their cooking. A ham hock is an example of this—it comes from just above the ankle of a pig. African American cooks used ham hocks to flavor collard greens, mustard greens, and beans, especially black-eyed peas. (Yes, black-eyed peas are actually beans!)

Directions:

1. Drain the water off the soaked black-eyed peas. Rinse them and drain again.

2. Place the black-eyed peas in a large, heavy pot. Add the ham hocks, onion, and garlic. Pour in just enough chicken stock or water to barely cover the ingredients.

Ingredients:

1 pound black-eyed peas, soaked in water for 8–24 hours

2 ham hocks

1 cup chopped onion

1 tablespoon minced garlic

6–8 cups unsalted chicken stock or water

1 or 2 chopped jalapeños (optional)

2 teaspoons seasoned salt

½ teaspoon sugar

Salt and black pepper

Cooked white rice

You Will Need:

Measuring cups and spoons

Large, heavy pot with lid

Wooden spoon

Cutting board

Sharp knife

3. Place the pot over medium-high heat. Bring the ingredients to a simmer. You may see some dark foam forming on the surface—just spoon it off until it's all gone. Then lower the heat so that the black-eyed peas simmer slowly. Simmer them, uncovered or partially covered, until they are nearly tender. This will take 45–60 minutes.

4. Remove the ham hocks and place them on a cutting board to cool. When the ham hocks are cool, pull the meat off them. Discard the bones and fat. Chop up the meat and put it back into the pot with the black-eyed peas.

5. Stir in the jalapeños (1 or both, depending on how spicy you like it, or none at all if you prefer), seasoned salt, and sugar into the pot. Partially cover the pot and simmer until the black-eyed peas are tender. This will take another 20–30 minutes. Taste the peas and add some salt and pepper, if you like.

6. Use a wooden spoon to smash some of the peas against the sides of the pot (doing this will thicken the mixture). Or leave it a little soupy, if you prefer. Serve with white rice.

Caution

Be sure to use plastic gloves when you are working with jalapeños.

Flavors from Backyards and Gardens

EVERYONE LIVING IN WISCONSIN knows that we have longer, darker winters and shorter growing seasons than people to the south of us. Perhaps that's why we love to be outdoors as long as the sun is shining. And that's why gardening is so important to Wisconsinites. Raising our own food is a Wisconsin tradition. We are proud of our long heritage of planting and harvesting, and we enjoy eating vegetables grown in local gardens and backyards.

In chapters 3 and 4, you learned the history of the crops that farmers grew for market and found recipes that use those foods. In this chapter, you'll learn about the ingredients and dishes that come from backyard, family, and community garden plots. Vegetables that are grown closer to home taste better to us. Perhaps we can taste our hard work as well as the delicious flavor of fresh produce!

But what if you don't have any outdoor gardening space? You can grow almost anything, from tomatoes to peppers to lettuce, in containers on a balcony, porch, or door stoop.

You can visit this re-created Danish garden at the Pederson house at Old World Wisconsin, a historic site near Eagle.

First Gardens

Native gardeners who lived in Wisconsin for thousands of years before Europeans set foot on the North American continent were masters at growing corn, beans, and squash. In fact, some Indian tribes called these crops the "three sisters." These Indians always planted these three crops together, partly because a legend said that the "three sisters" were always together, and partly because these plants grow very well when planted near each other. Our continent's first gardeners tilled their gardens with wooden plows and hoes or with garden tools made from the bones of large deer.

A Ho-Chunk woman shucked corn in this 1920 photograph.

Indians used ripe corn in many ways. Indians in the Green Bay area, for example, made a kind of corn cake from "green," or fresh, corn. (Green means that it's undried and unprocessed.) Cooks sliced the kernels off the cob and kneaded them into a paste. Then they formed this paste into small cakes. Finally, they wrapped the cakes in leaves and cooked them over hot coals.

Ho-Chunk women roasted green corn by covering large heated stones with corn husks. Next, they placed the corncobs on the stones and covered them with more husks. After the corn was roasted, the women cut the corn from the cob and dried it in the sun. They used this dried green corn for making soup. Once the green corn was dried, it would keep for years.

Wisconsin Indian people also made cornmeal. They ground dried corn in a wooden bowl using a large wooden pounder. Then they used the cornmeal to make porridge, which is a kind of cereal like oatmeal. They also used cornmeal to make simple bread cooked over an open fire. Indian women taught the first European settlers about cornmeal and cornbread. Later on, the Europeans added things that they were familiar with, such as milk and butter, to the bread. Europeans also traded these dairy products for Indian corn and other foods like wild rice and game meat.

The Menominee roasted or parched what they called *nanisa'pimin*, the variety of corn that we call popcorn. They pounded the nanisa'pimin into a coarse meal after it dried. They often mixed this with dried venison, maple sugar, or wild rice (or all three of these). Hunters or travelers carried this nourishing, lightweight mixture called pemmican. They ate pemmican dry or added water to it. You might say that pemmican was one of the original "to-go" foods.

Since Indian times, families have grown vegetables in home gardens. Corn quickly became a favorite food for the Europeans who arrived in Wisconsin, just as it did for those who found this Native food in other parts of the country. Although today you see corn growing in large fields on farms (often the type grown as feed for dairy cows), corn has also been a favorite thing to plant in backyard or community garden plots.

Belle La Follette, whose husband, Robert, was a U.S. senator known as "Fighting Bob," worked the garden of the family's farm in Maple Bluff in the early 1900s.

Immigrant Gardens

In their home countries in the 1800s, immigrants carefully and thoughtfully planned and packed for their new lives. They took with them just the things that they would need for the farms and homes they wanted to make in America. They packed seeds, roots, and cuttings of plants that they hoped would grow and nourish their families. They planned on growing vegetables for food, herbs for healing, and flowers for beauty.

Once they arrived in Wisconsin, every immigrant family—whether they got here 150 years ago or last week—had problems to face if they planned to grow food for themselves. They brought their own experiences and traditions of gardening with them. But they had to *learn* about the climate and soil of Wisconsin, and about the length of the growing season in the part of the state where they were living. In other words, these newcomers needed to adapt their techniques and knowledge to meet the demands of this new environment.

In the summer of 1936, Mr. Liebenberg had to stand on a ladder to measure the 14-foot tomato plant growing in his Madison garden.

The Koehler family in Phillips planted their garden in front of their newly built wooden house. Look at the size of that cabbage!

The Gardens at Old World Wisconsin

Today we can see examples of early immigrant gardens at Old World Wisconsin, the Wisconsin Historical Society's living history museum near Eagle. At Old World, visitors can see the way 12 different groups of immigrants farmed and lived in the 1800s. The homes of immigrant families like the Schulzes, the Kvaales, and the Kruzas were moved from their original locations around the state to Old World Wisconsin.

In front of the Schulz family's home, for example, you can see how they laid out their German-style kitchen garden neatly in rectangular blocks. The straight paths between the beds make it look like a patchwork quilt. In addition to their large kitchen garden, the Schulzes planted lots of cabbage and potatoes in their farm fields near Watertown to store for their winter needs. And they and other German settlers used some vegetables as medicines. They even used turnip juice to treat chicken pox!

The pumpkins and corn that are native to the Americas were new to Norwegians and other European immigrants. Norwegians found that both crops grew well and provided valuable food for their animals. Anders Ellingsen Kvaale left Norway for Wisconsin in 1848 with his wife, Christina, and their eight children. He made a lot of money selling the wool from the sheep he raised on his 160-acre farm in Dane County. But the family thought that corn and pumpkins were not very healthy for people so they never ate them. The Kvaales did use torn dried cornhusks to make mattress stuffing.

Polish settlers in Wisconsin placed a high value on root crops that they could store for winter. These included potatoes, beets, carrots, celeriac or celery root, parsley root, parsnips, rutabagas, and turnips. Polish families also liked to add horseradish, a root crop that is very hot in flavor, to sauces and soups. They believed it cleared their sinuses. Polish immigrants August and Barbara Kruza's house, originally built in Shawano County, is now at Old World Wisconsin. Their garden was close by and their chicken coop was under the same roof as their one-room log cabin. Gathering eggs was very convenient!

Visit Old World Wisconsin during the growing season to see how Wisconsin's early settlers planted their gardens and used their harvest to help them survive life in a new land.

Here's the Schulz Garden at Old World Wisconsin—a wonderful garden to visit while you're there. The Schulz family was from Pomerania in what is now Germany.

They also had to get used to unfamiliar foods so they could grow them in their gardens. Pumpkins and corn were two of the crops native to the Americas that were new to European immigrants. Imagine how strange a cob of corn must have seemed to a settler who had never seen such a vegetable before! At first, immigrant settlers raised foods they knew from their own countries. Each immigrant group planted its gardens with the flavors needed to make traditional foods. For example, most German immigrants could not imagine a garden without chives to add to their egg dishes. English and Scottish pioneers often favored sage, while families from all over northern Europe planted dill for their pickles. More recent Mexican and Hmong immigrants add cilantro from their gardens to many of their tasty dishes.

Root cellars like this one often had dirt floors and stone or brick walls. They provided families a cool, dark place to store long-lasting garden produce, like potatoes and pumpkins.

The early settlers planted the largest portion of their gardens with potatoes, onions, and other root crops that could be stored for the winter. Over time, however, they also learned how to cultivate and harvest (and enjoy!) native foods like corn and squash.

Settlers to Wisconsin in the 1830s and 1840s needed ways to store food over the winter. They didn't have grocery stores where they could buy their food during the cold months, so they preserved fruits and vegetables from their gardens and meats from their barnyard. There are many ways to preserve food. For example, cucumbers can be pickled and beets can be canned. Fish can be smoked and mushrooms can be dried. Many fruits and vegetables will keep for weeks, or even months, if they are packed in the right kind of container and kept in a cool place. And of course, most kinds of food can now be frozen.

But remember: pioneer families didn't have conveniences like freezers. They stored foods by hanging them from rafters, packing them into crocks, or smoking them, as with hams. Then home canning in glass jars took off in the 1860s with the 1858 invention of the mason jar with the threaded lid. Canning allowed people to preserve as much of their garden produce as possible so they could have vegetables all winter.

Successful gardeners have lots of produce to "put up," or can, as this Milwaukee woman knew so well back in 1961.

Add to your ration - by
Home Canning!
A 'V' HOME DOES !

THIS IS A
V
HOME

A victory garden added nutritious food for families on the home front during World War II, as this 1943 poster suggests. Many large farms sent their produce to feed fighting soldiers.

Community Gardens

Today, when people in towns and cities don't have enough space of their own—or enough sunny spots—to grow vegetables, sometimes they plant garden plots in community gardens. Community gardens have been around in Wisconsin since the early 20th century. During World Wars I and II, the governments of the countries at war worried that not enough food could be grown to feed both the people at home and the soldiers fighting. "Victory gardens" became a popular answer to the problem.

To help the war effort, many people created garden plots in their yards and on public lands, such as parks. People who planted victory gardens felt good knowing that growing their own food also gave them a way to help the troops fighting in the war. Victory gardens were a big success. By the time World War II ended, in 1945, 20 million Americans had planted a victory garden.

Grow Your Own
FRUITS AND VEGETABLES
Food Will Win the War and Write the Peace
Secretary, U.S. Department of Agriculture

Save ALL YOU RAISE
★ ★ ★
BUY UNITED STATES WAR BONDS AND STAMPS
INTERNATIONAL HARVESTER

Wisconsin has a long tradition of creating community gardens to help feed those in need. This boy liked helping with Madison's Community Chest Garden in 1949.

But when the war ended, so did the community victory gardens. Around the same time, more people had refrigerators with freezers and began buying frozen vegetables, which were new products in supermarkets. Then, in more and more families, both moms and dads began working outside the home, and people began eating more prepackaged or fast-food meals. Even though these were not the healthiest choices, they were quick and convenient, which is what many families wanted and needed. For several decades, fewer people spent time raising their own vegetables.

You learned in chapter 3 that in the 1990s people began to pay more attention to where their food came from. Buying and eating locally grown foods became more important. The idea of "eating local" became even more popular in the early 2000s.

As more people choose to eat locally, once again more families are creating gardens of all kinds all across Wisconsin. Those who live in apartments or have no space to make a home garden can participate in community gardens. Community gardens are similar to the victory gardens of years ago, but now they are popping up all over the place: in parks or other open public spaces, on the grounds of day-care centers and schools, or in the land around local community centers.

This little girl is watering the Boys and Girls Club's garden plot in the Marlborough community gardens in south Madison.

Got Dirt?

A different kind of community garden helps children learn how to make healthier eating choices. The Wisconsin Department of Health Services began a program known as Got Dirt? to train teachers of young children and those who work in child care to start gardens right at their schools and buildings. The Got Dirt? program has created hundreds of gardens in Wisconsin. One such garden is called a Microfarm, where the whole garden is planted on a wagon. The Microfarm allows students to garden in their own classrooms, even during Wisconsin's long, cold winters.

Worms make rich soil, and rich soil grows terrific vegetables.

One of the oldest community gardens in the United States is the Eagle Heights garden, just west of the University of Wisconsin campus in Madison. Eagle Heights residents come from all over the world to study at the university, and their gardens reflect the kinds of vegetables that are important to their own food traditions. In 2010, 53 garden plots covered 35 acres at Eagle Heights. And community gardens are being created in other Wisconsin cities and towns, large and small. The gardens that more recent immigrants to Wisconsin have planted continue to reflect their gardening heritage, just as earlier immigrant gardens did.

When the Madison Children's Museum moved into a new home in 2010, museum staff turned the rooftop into a year-round space for playing and learning. The space includes raised garden beds where children can plant seeds and harvest vegetables. They can also preserve or eat foods from the garden. There's a greenhouse where children can plant seeds even when they can't do so outdoors.

Will Allen's Growing Power in Milwaukee (see page 72) inspired the Madison Children's Museum to be a place where children can get firsthand experience in learning where and how we get our healthy, fresh food. Children even have the chance to feed and watch a small flock of chickens and collect their eggs from a rooftop chicken coop.

The rooftop garden at the Madison Children's Museum is a popular place during the summer.

Backyard Barnyards

From the time the first non-Indian settlers moved to Wisconsin to farm, they brought chickens with them. Those settlers who lived in towns also kept chickens in coops in their yards. Eggs are a great and easy source of protein.

Raising small flocks of chickens in urban backyards has become popular again in many Wisconsin communities. Families find that knowing exactly where they're getting fresh eggs makes a difference in their food habits. And eggs that can be gathered right in a backyard provide a healthy source of protein to families who don't have to leave home to find it. Children learn that taking care of a small flock of egg-laying hens is a bit like living on a farm.

Raising chickens in urban backyards means fresh eggs for many families. This chicken is a Silver Sebright named Laru.

Spider Johnnycake

8 servings

This is a modern spider, ready for an outdoor cookout!

This recipe shows how the foods from the Indians and the Europeans combined to create a new food. Johnnycake is Indian cornbread made with European dairy products. It's very moist and very good. Sometimes families cooked johnnycake in a pan called a "spider." This kind of spider is a cast-iron skillet that has legs on the bottom so it can be placed right over hot coals. For this recipe, you can use a regular cast-iron pan instead and bake the bread in the oven.

Directions:

1. Turn the oven to 375 degrees. Place the skillet in the oven. Let the pan heat up while you make the batter for the cornbread.

2. To make the batter, place the cornmeal, flour, sugar, baking powder, and salt in a large bowl.

3. Break 2 of the eggs into a smaller bowl. Use a whisk or an electric mixer to beat the eggs until they are smooth. Then beat in the milk until it is well combined with the eggs.

4. Pour the egg mixture into the flour mixture and gently stir until the 2 are just combined—mixing the batter too much will give the cornbread a tough texture when it's baked.

Recipes from Backyards and Gardens

Ingredients:

1 cup yellow cornmeal

⅓ cup flour

¼ cup sugar

2 teaspoons baking powder

1 teaspoon salt

3 eggs, divided

1 cup milk

1 cup half-and-half

2 tablespoons butter or lard

You Will Need:

8- or 9-inch cast-iron skillet

Measuring cups and spoons

Large and small bowls

Whisk or electric mixer

Wooden spoon

Thick towel

Oven mitts

Toothpicks

5. Beat the remaining egg in the smaller bowl. Add the half-and-half and beat well with the whisk or mixer. Set this aside.

6. Put a thick, folded towel on your worktable. Put on 2 oven mitts and remove the hot skillet from the oven, placing it on the towel. Add the butter or lard to the skillet. Tip the pan a little so that the melting butter covers the whole bottom of the pan.

7. Now pour the batter from the big bowl into the hot pan and use a wooden spoon to spread it out evenly (but don't stir it). It will sizzle a little—that means it's forming a nice crust on the bottom.

8. Carefully pour the egg mixture evenly over the top. Place the skillet back in the oven and bake the bread about 30 minutes. To test if it's done, stick a toothpick near the center of the cornbread and then remove the toothpick. If it comes out clean, the bread is done. If there's a little moist batter on the toothpick, keep baking it for a few more minutes. When the johnnycake is done, cool it on a wire rack. You can serve it warm or at room temperature. To serve, cut it into wedges, like a pie.

Corn on the Cob

Any number of servings

What's your favorite vegetable? If it's corn on the cob, you are in good company. From the ancient Indians who roasted fresh corn in outdoor pits to modern families who boil it in pots on the stove, people in Wisconsin have been enjoying corn for hundreds (even thousands!) of years.

Here are two methods for cooking corn on the cob. Take your pick of corn-on-the-cob toppings from the list below. Or dream up a new kind of topping of your own. What would taste good to you on corn?

Directions—Method 1:

1. Prepare a wood or charcoal fire on an outdoor grill. Or, heat a gas-fired grill to medium-hot.

2. Pull down—but do not remove!—the husks from ears of fresh corn.

3. Now pull off the white "silk" from the corn. Get as much of it off as you can.

4. Fold the husks back up around the corn. Twist the tops to help them stay closed.

5. Place the ears of corn in a bucket of water and let them soak for 10 minutes.

6. When the fire is ready, remove the ears from the water and use tongs to place them on the hot grill.

7. Grill the corn for about 20–25 minutes. Turn the ears occasionally as they grill. The husks will get a little burned and crusty looking, but that's okay.

This boy enjoyed delicious, buttery corn on the cob at the Sun Prairie Sweet Corn Festival, held each August.

Caution

Be sure an adult is working with you for this method!

Ingredients:

Fresh corn on the cob

Topping ideas:

Butter and salt

Mayonnaise and grated
Parmesan cheese

Olive oil and drops of lemon juice

Pesto

Sour cream and
chopped fresh chives

Barbecue sauce

You Will Need:

For Method 1:
Charcoal or gas-fired outdoor grill
Clean bucket
Large barbecue tongs

For Method 2:
Aluminum foil
Teaspoon

8. Let the corn cool a little and then remove the husks.

9. Add your favorite toppings to the corn and dig in.

Directions—Method 2:

1. Heat the oven to 400 degrees.

2. Pull off the husks and all the silky threads from the corn.

3. Place each ear of corn on a square of aluminum foil.

4. Sprinkle a teaspoon of water on each ear.

5. Wrap each ear tightly in the foil.

6. Bake 30 minutes. Be careful when you open the corn packets! Some hot steam
will come out.

7. Add your favorite toppings to the corn and eat it up.

Baked Squash or Pumpkin

From the first Indian tribes who lived near the Great Lakes to young families who want to eat local foods today, people in Wisconsin have been preserving food for a very long time. With our cold winters, it is good to know that we can eat well even when our gardens are not growing.

Here are two methods for preserving pumpkin and other types of winter squash, such as butternut and acorn squash.

Winter squash comes in many colorful varieties. Try them all to see how the flavors differ.

Cool Storage Squash:

Winter squashes that are harvested in the fall in Wisconsin will keep for 2 to 4 months if you store them the right way. First, you need squashes that are very firm and heavy and don't have any cuts or soft spots on them. (Summer squashes like zucchini will not work.) Make sure you are storing squashes that still have their stems on—this helps them keep better. Place them in a box in a single layer and store them in a cool, dry location. The best place is a fruit cellar (a small, dark room with shelves) in the basement, but an attic that is well insulated will also work. The best kinds of squash to store this way are the really hard ones with dark orange flesh, like butternut or Hubbard squash. In fact, these varieties will taste better after they have been stored for a few weeks!

Frozen Squash Puree:

Another way to store winter squash is to bake it (like a potato), mash the cooked flesh, and then freeze it in containers or freezer bags. This will work for almost any kind of winter squash, even pumpkins. (If you do use pumpkins, they should be "pie pumpkins," the kind that are grown for eating—not Halloween pumpkins, which are for scaring people!)

First, rinse them well. Then, being very careful, poke each one in 3 or 4 places with a strong fork or a small, sharp knife. Line a baking pan with aluminum foil and bake them at 350 degrees until they become really soft. This will take 1½–2 hours, depending on how big the squash are.

When the squashes come out of the oven, split them open so they can cool down. When they are cool enough for you to handle, pull out the seeds and membranes. Now take a spoon and scrape all the flesh off the rinds. Place the flesh in a food processor or blender. Blend until the squash is smooth—this is called a puree. (Some people just use a spoon or fork to mash the squash.)

Make sure the squash puree is completely cool before you freeze it. Spoon it into containers with tight-fitting lids, but fill them only three-quarters full. Put the lids on tightly. It's also a good idea to put a label on each container so that when you want to use your pureed squash, you will know which container it's in!

Pureed squash can be used in soups, pies, and cookies (see recipe on page 140). Or just heat it up with some butter, salt, and pepper.

You Will Need:

Strong fork or small, sharp knife
Baking pan
Aluminum foil
Large spoon
Food processor or blender
Containers with tight-fitting lids
Labels or markers

Caution

This recipe calls for the use of a food processor, which has very sharp blades. Be sure an adult is present and watching closely when you are handling the food processor.

Pumpkin Cookies

40–48 cookies

Squash is an ancient food in Wisconsin. (And yes, pumpkins are squashes!) This recipe was adapted from one in *From Asparagus to Zucchini: A Guide to Farm-Fresh Seasonal Produce* (Madison Area Community Supported Agriculture Coalition, 2003).

Directions:

1. Heat oven to 350 degrees. Grease 2 large cookie sheets or line them with parchment paper.

2. Place butter and brown sugar in a large bowl. Use a wooden spoon to beat them together until creamy and smooth. Mix in the pumpkin, eggs, and vanilla. Stir until everything is well blended.

3. In another bowl, combine the flour, baking soda, cinnamon, nutmeg, cloves, and salt. Use a whisk to stir them together thoroughly.

You could make a lot of pumpkin cookies from a 93-pound pumpkin!

Ingredients:

2 sticks (1 cup) softened butter

1¼ cups brown sugar

2 cups cooked pumpkin puree
(see page 139 for instructions)

2 large eggs

1 teaspoon vanilla extract

4¾ cups flour

2 teaspoons baking soda

2 teaspoons ground cinnamon

2 teaspoons ground nutmeg

½ teaspoon ground cloves

½ teaspoon salt

½ cup chopped dried cherries or dried
cranberries (optional)

You Will Need:

2 large cookie sheets

Parchment paper (optional)

2 large bowls

Measuring cups and spoons

Wooden spoon

Whisk

Spatula

Wire cooling racks

Oven mitts

4. Add the flour mixture to the pumpkin mixture. Stir to combine. Stir in the dried cherries or dried cranberries (or you can leave these out if you want).

5. Drop the cookie dough by spoonfuls onto the prepared cookie sheets. The little mounds of cookie dough should be at least 2 inches apart.

6. Bake 15 minutes. When the cookies are done, use a spatula (and oven mitts on your hands!) to transfer the cookies to wire racks. Let them cool off before you eat them . . . if you can wait that long!

Fresh Corn and Tomato Salsa

3–4 cups

Salsa is a spicy tomato dip or sauce that originally came from Mexico and Central America. Immigrants who came north from those regions introduced North Americans to salsa. Today salsa is popular all across the United States, including in Wisconsin.

There are many, many different recipes for salsa. This one features tomatoes, corn, and other vegetables that grow in Wisconsin gardens—plus avocados, a fruit that grows in tropical climates. (Luckily, you can buy these yummy pear-shaped treats at most grocery stores!)

Directions:

1. Place the corn kernels in a bowl.

2. Cut the tomatoes into slices, then cut the slices into small chunks. Add them to the corn.

3. Finely chop the green pepper and add it to the bowl.

4. Cut the avocado in half and remove the pit and peel. Finely chop the avocado flesh and add it to the bowl.

5. Finely chop the green onions. Add them to the bowl.

How to Cut and Peel an Avocado

Avocados contain large, hard pits. It's good to know this when you want to cut one, because trying to cut through a hard pit is not a good idea! Instead, use a small, sharp knife to cut into the peel until it reaches the pit (you'll feel the knife stop). Now continue to cut through the peel to the pit in a single line all around the whole avocado. This will divide the avocado into 2 sections. Twist the 2 sections to open up the avocado. Now cut each half-section into 2 more sections. Pull the peels off all the sections. Now you can chop the peeled avocado sections into pieces.

Ingredients:

1 cup corn kernels (cut fresh off the cob or frozen and thawed)

3 medium-sized tomatoes (heirloom varieties often taste the best!)

1 small green pepper

1 ripe avocado

2 green onions

1 jalapeño pepper

¼ cup cilantro or basil leaves

1 lime

1 tablespoon olive oil or corn oil

½ teaspoon salt

⅛ teaspoon black pepper

Tortilla chips

You Will Need:

Large bowl

Knife

Cutting board

Plastic gloves (optional)

Measuring cups and spoons

Wooden spoon

6. Next you're going to chop the jalapeño pepper. IMPORTANT: The juice of jalapeños can sting your fingers, so wear plastic kitchen gloves if you have them, or if you don't, be sure to wash your hands after you handle the pepper (be especially careful not to touch your eyes after handling a hot pepper!). Finely chop the jalapeño. Add to the salsa.

7. Chop the cilantro or basil leaves and add them to the salsa.

8. Cut the lime in half and squeeze the juice into the salsa.

9. Add the oil, salt, and pepper to the salsa. Mix well.

10. You can eat the salsa right away or let it stand for 15–30 minutes to develop more flavor. Serve the salsa with tortilla chips.

Caution

Be sure to use plastic gloves when you are working with jalapeños.

Tomato Salad with International Flavor

4 servings

Local farmers' market tomatoes are the best!

There is a big difference between the pale, packaged tomatoes found at the grocery store and the ones picked fresh from a garden or purchased from a farmers' market. Garden tomatoes are picked fresh, so they have lots of flavor and nutrition. Many grocery-store tomatoes are picked before they are ripe, so that they stay firm and can be packaged for shipping. Try a side-by-side taste experiment sometime and see which you like better.

Many of the best-tasting tomatoes are heirloom types. Heirlooms are older varieties of tomatoes and they come in different shapes, sizes, and colors. Some are yellow, some are red, some are pink, and some are green. Some are even kind of purple. Growers raise heirloom tomatoes for their delicious flavors. Many heirloom varieties have been grown for a hundred or more years. You know a tomato must be delicious if people have been enjoying it for a hundred years.

This is a simple tomato salad. You can change it by adding different flavor mixes to the salad. Each flavor mix represents a different immigrant group that came to Wisconsin.

Ingredients:

8 large or 14 medium tomatoes (select
different colors and shapes if you can)

Salt and black pepper

International Flavors

Italian:
1 tablespoon balsamic vinegar
2–3 tablespoons olive oil
2 tablespoons chopped fresh basil

German:
1 tablespoon apple cider vinegar
heated with 2 tablespoons bacon fat
1 tablespoon water
2 teaspoons sugar
3 tablespoons chopped fresh
green onion

French:
2 teaspoons tarragon vinegar
2 tablespoons walnut oil
1½ tablespoons minced shallot
1 teaspoon Dijon-style mustard

Norwegian:
1 tablespoon fresh lemon juice
¼ cup heavy cream
2 tablespoons chopped fresh
dill leaves

Mexican:
1 tablespoon fresh lime juice
2–3 tablespoons corn oil
2 tablespoons chopped fresh cilantro
1–2 teaspoons minced garlic

You Will Need:

Measuring cups and spoons
Knife
Cutting board
Serving platter

Directions:

1. Slice the tomatoes and arrange them on a platter. You can mix them up or group
them in little piles. Sprinkle the tomatoes with a little salt and pepper.

2. Mix up the international flavor of your choice. Drizzle the mixture over the
tomatoes. Serve the tomato salad at room temperature.

Chunky Pickled Garden Cukes

12 or more servings

Making pickles is a great way to preserve cucumbers. Pickles are made by soaking cucumbers in vinegar, sugar, and spices. Pickling used to be much more common in Wisconsin than it is now. Today we can buy pickles at the grocery store. But in past centuries, pickling was an important way to stock up on food.

Cucumbers are the pickles we know best, but many kinds of vegetables and fruits can be pickled. In the past, families even pickled things like watermelon rinds and corncobs. These pickled cukes will keep in the refrigerator for many weeks.

This Polish family harvested cucumbers in Sobieski, Wisconsin, in 1943.

Ingredients:

8 cups chunked or thick-sliced cucumber (unpeeled)

1 tablespoon salt

1 cup chopped onion

1 cup chopped sweet red bell pepper

2 cups sugar

1 cup cider vinegar

1 teaspoon celery seeds

1 teaspoon mustard seeds

You Will Need:

Large bowl with cover (or plastic wrap) and medium bowl

Colander

Measuring cups and spoons

Wooden spoons

Directions:

1. Put the cucumbers in a large bowl and toss them with the salt. Let the cucumbers stand for 1 hour.

2. Drain (but do not rinse) the cukes in a colander and press them lightly to get the extra liquid out. Clean and dry the bowl. Place the cukes back in the bowl.

3. Stir in the onion and bell pepper.

4. In a separate bowl, combine the sugar, vinegar, celery seeds, and mustard seeds. Stir well until all the sugar is dissolved. Pour over cucumber mixture and stir everything together. Cover the bowl and put it in the refrigerator for 2 to 3 days, to develop flavor.

Butter-Glazed Carrot Coins with Fresh Mint

8–10 servings

Immigrants grew more than vegetables in their gardens. They grew herbs, too, and added them to many dishes. Mint is an herb many immigrants enjoyed. They used it to make tea, but also to season carrots and other vegetables.

Directions:

1. Place about 10 cups water in a pot. Add the salt. Cover and bring the water to a boil.

2. While the water is heating, peel the carrots, then slice them into rounds, each about ¼ inch thick.

3. Chop up the mint.

4. When the water comes to a boil, add the carrots. Boil uncovered 2–3 minutes, then drain the carrots.

5. Heat the butter in a skillet over medium heat. When the butter begins to sizzle a little, add the drained carrots, sugar, and mint. Stir, cooking the carrots until they are tender and look glazed and shiny.

Ingredients:

10 cups water

1 tablespoon salt

1 pound carrots

¼ cup fresh mint leaves

4 tablespoons butter

¼ cup sugar

You Will Need:

4-quart saucepan with lid
Measuring cups and spoons
Sharp knife
Cutting board
Colander or strainer
Skillet
Wooden spoon

If someone you know has a mint plant, try picking a leaf and crushing it between your fingers. Then take a sniff!

Chocolate-Dipped Strawberries

40–48 dipped berries

With or without chocolate, strawberries are a wonderful taste of summer.

In this chapter you learned about the backyard vegetable gardens of the past and present. Gardeners, however, also grow *fruits* in their backyards, of course. Strawberry patches provide "fast food" snacks ("fast food" because all you have to do is go outside and pick them!), and rhubarb plants supply plenty of their tart fruit for pies. Some fruits aren't part of the garden; instead, they grow on a tree in the front yard— such as apples or plums—or in bushes along the side of the house, such as raspberries or blackberries. Homegrown fruits are part of what make life in Wisconsin sweet.

Directions:

1. Gently rinse the strawberries. Let them dry on paper towels.

2. Line a large baking sheet or tray with waxed paper. Set aside.

Ingredients:

2 quarts whole, stem-on large, fresh
strawberries

1½ cups chocolate chips

4½ tablespoons butter,
cut into small pieces

You Will Need:

Paper towels
Large baking sheet or tray
Waxed paper
Double boiler (a pot that has a second,
smaller pot that fits inside of it)

3. Put some water in the bottom pot of the double boiler—enough to come about 2 inches up the sides of the pot. Fit the second pot inside it, over the water.

4. Place chocolate chips and butter pieces in the double boiler. Place over medium heat. Do not cover the double boiler. Heat the ingredients, without stirring, until melted. Remove from heat and stir until smooth.

5. Dip the strawberries into the chocolate one at a time, leaving the upper half uncoated. Place dipped berries on the lined tray. Chill in the refrigerator at least 10 minutes—this will make the chocolate firm up. Keep the berries chilled until ready to serve.

Schmorn

6 servings

Remember that most pioneer families raised chickens, and eggs were a regular ingredient in pioneer kitchens. They gathered fresh eggs every day and used them in many kinds of baked goods and dishes. Eggs were also a main dish for breakfast, lunch, or dinner.

Schmorn is an old-fashioned Slovenian (from Slovenia) main dish that is made from eggs. It comes from central Europe and is like a cross between pancakes and scrambled eggs. In the springtime, a pioneer family would eat this dish with a salad made from dandelion greens. The family could gather both the eggs and the dandelion leaves right from their own yard!

Directions:

1. Separate the egg into 2 bowls (see page 30 for instructions).

2. Add the milk and sugar to the egg yolks. Beat with an electric mixer or eggbeater until smooth. Add the flour, baking powder, and salt. Beat until smooth. Beat in the vanilla and lemon juice. Set aside.

3. Clean and dry the beaters very well. Now use them to beat the egg whites until they form stiff peaks.

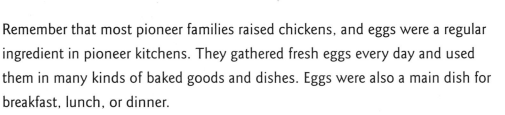

Many of Wisconsin's farmers used whatever eggs their family didn't eat to trade for other goods.

Ingredients:

4 large eggs

2 cups milk

¼ cup sugar

1 cup plus 3 tablespoons flour

1 teaspoon baking powder

½ teaspoon salt

1 teaspoon vanilla extract

1 teaspoon lemon juice

4 tablespoons butter

Jam or maple syrup (optional)

You Will Need:

Mixing bowls

Measuring cups and spoons

Electric mixer or handheld
  rotary eggbeater

Rubber spatula

Large skillet
  with lid

Metal or hard plastic spatula

4. Use a rubber spatula to fold the egg whites into the flour mixture (see page 31 for instructions). Don't beat them in! Be gentle.

5. Melt the butter in a large skillet over medium-high heat. Now add the batter and cook it until a crust begins to form on the bottom. Then cover the skillet and turn the heat down to very low. Let the mixture cook until it is about double in height. This will take 15–20 minutes.

6. Remove cover. Use a spatula to chop the schmorn into crumbly pieces, turning them over as you chop them. Keep turning the pieces over low heat until they are browned. Serve with jam or maple syrup, if you like.

CHAPTER 6

Flavors from Families and Communities

IN THE FIRST FIVE CHAPTERS of this book we have looked at how the food we eat comes from the environment of Wisconsin—our forests, waterways, fields, farms, and gardens. All of these are examples of the *places* our food comes from. But what about foods and recipes that come from *people*—from our families and our communities? How do the people of Wisconsin influence how and what we eat?

In this chapter, we'll explore the food traditions that answer these questions. A warning: it's impossible to talk about the food traditions of our families, our ancestors, and our communities without overlapping, since people brought their food traditions with them to Wisconsin and passed them on to their families and the communities in which they lived. That's one of the many things that make our state such an interesting place to live—and eat!

These girls dressed in Hmong finery for a Fourth of July celebration in Sheboygan.

Foods of Our Ancestors

In Wisconsin, many communities have their own special food traditions. For example, brats are popular all over the state, but Sheboygan thinks of itself as the brat capital. Milwaukee's south side probably has more Mexican food restaurants than anywhere else in the state. And Monroe is the only place in the entire country that makes smelly and creamy Limburger cheese. Why are those foods special to those communities?

The families who settled in these places brought their food traditions with them. Sheboygan was home to many German sausage-making families. Milwaukee's south side was once mostly Polish, but now the neighborhood has a large number of Mexican families. Swiss families settled in Monroe and brought their skills and taste for strong cheeses with them.

When you visit New Glarus, you can see the community's strong Swiss heritage, especially if you go to the town's yearly Wilhelm Tell Fest.

The entire German American Goldenberger family enjoyed this wurst roast near Madison in 1912.

During the late 1800s and early 1900s, millions of people migrated to the United States. They often created new communities made up mainly of people with the same ethnic background. Many of the people who settled in Wisconsin originally came from different parts of northern Europe. Wisconsin's largest group of immigrants came from Germany. If you look at the map, you can see that families from Germany made their homes throughout the state, although Milwaukee County is our most German area.

People from Poland arrived later and were the next largest group to settle in Wisconsin. Norwegians also settled in many communities. Some towns, like Stoughton and Westby, still have strong Norwegian traditions.

Other groups were smaller and settled more locally: Belgians in Green Bay and southern Door County, Dutch in communities south of Green Bay near the Fox River, Danes in Racine County, Swiss around New Glarus and Monroe, Finns along Lake Superior in Bayfield County. And these are only a few.

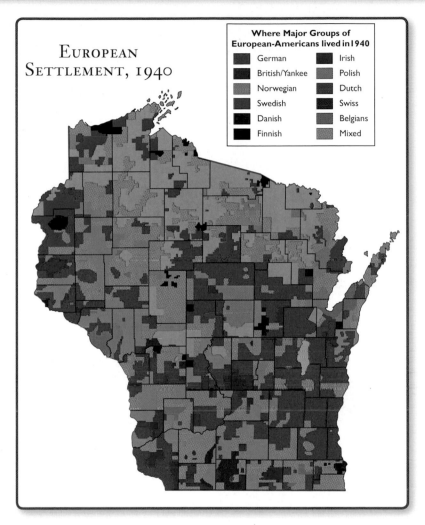

EUROPEAN SETTLEMENT, 1940

Where Major Groups of European-Americans lived in 1940

German	Irish
British/Yankee	Polish
Norwegian	Dutch
Swedish	Swiss
Danish	Belgians
Finnish	Mixed

No matter where they came from, immigrants brought along things that would remind them of home. This helped them get used to living in a new place. All of these groups brought with them their treasured recipes and food traditions. This means that over time, Wisconsin has become known for dishes that were first prepared in the home countries of our immigrant settlers.

Southern Flavors from the Pleasant Ridge Settlement

In 1848, former slaves founded a small farm community called Pleasant Ridge in Grant County in southwest Wisconsin. Pleasant Ridge also became the home of immigrant Europeans and European Americans. The children of all these families attended school together.

The African American families who settled at Pleasant Ridge brought with them their taste for southern cooking and eating. In the early years of the 1900s they organized the Autumn Leaf Club, which sponsored annual get-togethers to raise money. Chef Samuel C. Craig was for many years in charge of the food for the event. The morning of the gathering, he began roasting and frying large amounts of chicken and pork, and both the black and white members of the community would enjoy the large outdoor feast. The tradition continued up until World War II in the early 1940s. How nice it is to enjoy good food and friendship!

Neighbors in Pleasant Ridge, both black and white, built their community school and sent their children to attend. This photograph is from 1890.

Racine is known as home to Danish kringle, like this fresh-baked one at Howard's Bakery.

For instance, bakers in Racine make a wreath-shaped pastry called *kringle* that their ancestors in Denmark used to make. At restaurants in Mineral Point you can order a *pasty*, a small meat pie that Cornish miners used to pack in their lunch to take to the lead mines around southwestern Wisconsin. In the area around southern Door County and Green Bay, where many Belgian families settled, Catholic churches often serve Belgian pies and Belgian *trippe*, a sausage made from pork and cabbage. These are just a handful of the special dishes passed down from families who arrived in the state in the 1800s.

Flavors from Newer Arrivals

In the past 100 years, people from other countries and from other states have continued to make new homes in Wisconsin. Like the earlier immigrants, these newer arrivals to our state have also mostly settled together in the same areas.

In the early and mid-1900s, many African American families from the South came here for factory jobs in southern Wisconsin cities, especially Racine, Beloit, and Milwaukee. Many brought their taste for Southern cooking along with them.

Mexican Americans often came as migrant workers in the mid- to late 1900s. They helped Wisconsin farmers harvest their crops. Many chose to settle here and work year-round. Mexican Americans are Wisconsin's largest-growing Spanish-speaking community. Spanish speakers from other countries in Central and South America and Puerto Rico also have made Wisconsin their home.

Beginning in 1975, after the Vietnam War, many Lutheran churches in Minnesota and Wisconsin helped Hmong families from Southeast Asia settle in their states. In Wisconsin, the largest communities of Hmong people are in Milwaukee, Madison, Wausau, Sheboygan, Eau Claire, and La Crosse.

Many migrant workers, like this family, travel to Door County to pick cherries each summer.

As you will find in the recipes in this chapter, the immigrants and migrants who came to Wisconsin more recently have brought new flavors to the state. As you visit towns around the state, you will find family-owned Mexican, Thai, and Middle Eastern restaurants along with the supper clubs and local diners. The next time you go to the grocery store, notice how many different kinds of ingredients there are to make Indian or Asian dishes. And when you attend any kind of festival or gathering where there are good things to eat, look for foods from other places that are now "at home" in Wisconsin.

Gatherings and Celebrations

When we think of our own family's foodways, or food traditions, we might think of the things we eat on special occasions, like birthdays and holidays. Families often have special recipes and dishes that they make only during religious holidays, such as all kinds of fancy cookies at Christmas, ham at Easter, matzoh ball soup for Passover, or fig and lemon chicken as a big meal after the Ramadan fast. Families also might celebrate other holidays with special food traditions, like turkey at Thanksgiving or hot dogs on the Fourth of July.

The family of Abe and Sarah Mintz gathered to celebrate a Seder dinner back in 1945 in Madison. Passover is still the major home holiday for Jewish families.

Often, our families are also part of larger groups. Sometimes, these are religious groups, made up of people who belong to the same church, synagogue, or mosque, for example. When each of these groups of people gather together, they celebrate with special foods.

The tradition of the "church supper" (sometimes breakfast or lunch, too!) has been around a long time in Wisconsin. When those groups of early settlers began arriving here, they often shared not just their ethnic heritage but also their religion. Gathering together to enjoy a meal after church was a way for them to feel like a community. And eating the foods they loved in their homeland reminded them that they had something in common with each other here in a new land.

Friday Fish Fry

Have you ever been to a fish fry? Going out for fried fish on Fridays is a tradition for many families in Wisconsin. The Friday night fish fry takes place in many kinds of places—small cafés, big restaurants, neighborhood bars, supper clubs, and even church basements.

Friday fish fry is a Wisconsin tradition for a number of reasons. For one thing, as you learned in chapter 3, there are lots of lakes and rivers in Wisconsin, with plenty of fish. Eating fish is something people in the area have been doing for a long, long time.

But another reason fish fries became popular is that many of the immigrants who came here in the 1800s from Europe were Catholics. According to the rules of their church, Catholics did not eat meat on Fridays. They often ate fish on Fridays instead. They could get inexpensive meals of fish at local inns and taverns. Non-Catholics also liked these inexpensive meals of fish. It became a popular custom to take the whole family out for fish on Fridays.

Fish fries are the same wherever you go—but they're also different wherever you go. How can that be? At a fish fry, the fish is dipped in a batter and then deep-fried in hot oil. (Sometimes you get a choice of baked fish or fish fried in a shallow pan instead of deep-fried.) And a fish fry meal typically comes with potatoes, bread, coleslaw, and tartar sauce. All over the state people enjoy this same meal on Friday nights. But one restaurant might serve perch at its fish fry and another might serve cod. Some places give you a choice of different kinds of potatoes, or bread, or salad. So fish fries also are a little different from place to place.

Today a fish fry is more than a meal in Wisconsin. You might bump into friends or neighbors at a fish fry. It's a casual, friendly event. It's a little like a party—a party that everyone in the state is invited to, every Friday night.

Can't you hear this fish sizzling right on the plate?

Norwegian women prepare for a church supper. This photo is more than 50 years old, but new generations keep the church supper tradition alive all over Wisconsin.

These days, many of these church and community meals still feature those same foods. For example, many Norwegian immigrants were Lutherans, and to this day Norwegian Lutheran church gatherings all over the state feature Norwegian meatballs, *lutefisk* (cod that is dried, then soaked, and then boiled), and *lefse* (a soft, flat bread). Of course, church suppers and other community gatherings today probably also include foods from a mix of countries, especially when the gathering is a "potluck," meaning everyone brings their favorite dish to share.

Our families are also part of the larger community around us. You probably belong to several communities. The city or town you live in, the school you go to, and even the neighborhood around your house are communities.

You read earlier about how lots of Wisconsin's immigrants settled near each other, forming communities that shared cultural and food traditions. Some Wisconsin communities today are still so proud of their particular heritage that they host big parties where people can try their special foods, drinks, songs, and dances. These festivals happen all over the state and in all months of the year.

Festa Italiana is one of the many ethnic festivals held at Milwaukee's lakefront every summer.

For example, at the Czech-Slovak Community Festival in Phillips every June, visitors can sample the foods and other traditions of the Czech Republic and neighboring countries, including tasting homemade *kolacky,* a sweet pastry. At the annual Kermis Festival in Little Chute, people are invited to "be Dutch for a day" and enjoy a Dutch *pannekoeke,* or pancake, breakfast. The state's biggest city, Milwaukee, hosts the largest number of ethnic festivals. They include German Fest, African World Festival, Irish Fest, Festa Italiana (Italy), and Bastille Days (France), and they all feature delicious foods.

Oktoberfest in La Crosse honors our state's German cultural traditions.

Also in Milwaukee every fall is Indian Summer Festival, a huge celebration of Wisconsin's Native peoples. Many of Wisconsin's food traditions are closely tied to our Native Nations—the Ho-Chunk, Menominee, Potawatomi, Ojibwe, Mohican, Oneida, and Brothertown Indians. At Indian Summer Festival and at other powwows all around the state, Native people share their dance, craft, and food traditions. Fry bread and hull corn soup are favorite powwow foods that both Native and non-Native powwow visitors enjoy.

This 1920 photograph shows a Ho-Chunk woman preparing fry bread at the Indian Summer festival in Milwaukee or at powwows all over the state.

The town of Franksville celebrates its German heritage at Kraut Festival.

Not all of our food festivals are about our religious or ethnic background. Wisconsin people just love to get together and celebrate food! Some food fests feature crops that grow well in a particular area, like the annual Cranberry Festival (the "world's largest cranberry festival"!) in Warrens, Apple Fest in Bayfield, or Sweet Corn Festival in Sun Prairie.

As you learned in chapter 4, Wisconsin has been a dairy state for over 150 years, and there are many dairy celebrations here. At festivals like Green County Cheese Days in Monroe, you can watch cows being milked and taste many kinds of cheese, all made nearby. At the Great Wisconsin Cheese Festival in Little Chute, you can take part in a cheesecake-making contest. And every year in June—officially known as Dairy Month—there are dairy breakfasts at farms all over the state, where you can enjoy dairy treats along with your eggs and bacon. (Ice cream for breakfast? Hooray!)

Lucky boys have ice cream for their dairy breakfast in Ozaukee County!

Food festivals are times when people who belong to one group can celebrate what makes them special. But they also give people from *other* places or backgrounds the chance to taste new foods and flavors. From the huge ethnic fests in Milwaukee to church potluck suppers to a festival all about the cheese curd, these gatherings offer everyone a taste of Wisconsin's many cultures and traditions.

The Taste of Home

Now that you're thinking about the many exciting and delicious food traditions going on all around Wisconsin, remember that some of the best eating happens right in your own kitchen. Family food traditions are going on all the time, not just on holidays and special occasions. Whether you start your school day with eggs or cold cereal for breakfast, pack peanut butter and jelly sandwiches or sushi in your lunchbox, make macaroni and cheese from scratch or from a box at dinner, or sit down to hot pancakes and syrup every Sunday morning, you are eating according to your own family's food traditions.

This farm family knew that the food might be plain, but everybody would have enough to eat, and nobody complained.

Now that you've paid more attention to where our foods come from—the natural environment of Wisconsin and the foods our families and ancestors brought with them—it's time to gather some of the recipes from your own family! Who's the main cook in your home? Are there dishes that you already love to eat that are the specialties of some family member or friend? If there's a chance that you can learn to cook and spend time in the kitchen with an older family member, you'll find that the stories and memories of preparing those foods are as much a part of eating them as the foods themselves. Maybe you'll create your own notebook of "favorite flavors" that you can add to as you taste new foods. When you write down the recipes, be sure to write some of the stories that go along with the foods!

These women are making Norwegian sandbakkels, or sand tarts, rich cookies rolled in powdered sugar and sure to please! Does your family have a favorite cookie recipe?

Norwegian Meatballs

10–12 servings

The annual Syttende Mai celebration in Stoughton includes a children's parade.

Westby and Stoughton are two of the many towns in Wisconsin that celebrate their Norwegian heritage. Residents and visitors celebrate during *Syttende Mai,* which is Norwegian for May 17, Norway's Independence Day. Norwegian meatballs are one of the dishes eaten for Syttende Mai. The meatballs are usually served with mashed potatoes and coleslaw.

Directions:

1. Put the ground beef, ground pork, onion, eggs, breadcrumbs, and milk in a large bowl. Add the salt, sugar, and nutmeg.

2. Use your (clean!) heads to mix everything well. Let the mixture stand 15 minutes.

3. Now roll the mixture into balls, each one about the size of a small plum. If the mixture is too sticky, wet your hands a little first.

4. Add enough oil to a large, heavy skillet to come ¼ inch up the sides. Heat the oil over medium heat while you flour the meatballs.

5. To flour the meatballs: Place some flour (about a cup) in a medium bowl. Put the meatballs, a few at a time, in the flour. Turn them over until they are lightly coated with the flour. Take them out 1 at a time, shake them off, and put them on a plate.

Ingredients:

1½ pounds ground beef

¼ pound ground pork sausage

½ cup minced onion

3 eggs

½ cup dried breadcrumbs

¼ cup milk

1 teaspoon salt

1 teaspoon sugar

¼ teaspoon nutmeg

Canola oil (enough to come ¼ inch up the sides of the skillet)

1 cup flour

1 can (10¾ ounces) cream of mushroom soup

1 cup beef or chicken broth

You Will Need:

Measuring cups and spoons

Large and medium bowls

Plate

Large, heavy skillet

Tongs for turning the meatballs

Paper towels

Large baking dish

Wooden spoon

6. Check to see if the oil is hot enough. It's hot enough if it sizzles as soon as you put a sprinkle of flour in it.

7. Fry the meatballs in batches—do not crowd the pan. Turn the meatballs once or twice as they cook. Cook them until they are browned. Drain each batch on paper towels.

8. Heat oven to 350 degrees. Place all the browned meatballs in a large baking dish.

9. Pour off all the oil from the skillet. Add the mushroom soup and broth to the skillet. Bring this sauce to a simmer, stirring often.

10. Pour sauce over meatballs. Bake 50–60 minutes. Gently stir the meatballs once or twice as they bake. The sauce will get thicker as it cooks.

Worstenbroodjes (Dutch "Pigs in a Blanket")

12–14 rolls

These small, savory rolls are popular at the annual Holland Festival in Cedar Grove, Wisconsin, a former fishing village that is very proud of its Dutch heritage.

You can easily double or triple this recipe. If you do, you should still bake them one batch at a time so they cook properly.

Directions:

1. Heat the oven to 350 degrees. Unwrap the can of dough and unroll the dough on your work surface. You will have 4 rectangles of dough, each about 4 inches by 7 inches. Depending on the size of the sausages, you should be able to make 3 or 4 worstenbroodjes from each dough rectangle.

2. Pat each dough rectangle nice and flat, and use your fingers to press together any seams to close them up. Don't press too hard—press just enough to smooth the dough.

3. Lay one sausage on the short end of a dough rectangle. Fold the dough up and over the ends of the sausage. (You can stretch the dough a little to do this.) Holding the dough over the ends of the sausage, roll the sausage forward so it is completely covered in dough. Use the knife or pizza cutter to cut the dough along the length of the sausage. Pinch the dough together a little to seal it. You should have a sausage completely bundled inside dough. Place the sausage bundle seam-side down on a large baking sheet.

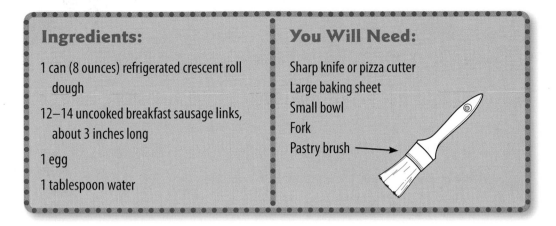

Ingredients:

1 can (8 ounces) refrigerated crescent roll dough

12–14 uncooked breakfast sausage links, about 3 inches long

1 egg

1 tablespoon water

You Will Need:

Sharp knife or pizza cutter

Large baking sheet

Small bowl

Fork

Pastry brush

4. Continue making bundles with the rest of the sausages and dough. If you have some scraps of dough left, you can pinch those together to make 1 or 2 more worstenbroodjes.

5. Beat the egg and water together in a small bowl. Use a pastry brush to brush a little of the egg mixture over the top of each sausage bundle. This will give the dough a nice glossy shine when it bakes.

6. Bake until golden brown, 18–22 minutes. Watch carefully so the bottoms don't get too brown.

Easy Cornish Pasties

4 servings

Cornish miners found that a pasty made a perfect noon meal.

Cornish immigrants came to southwestern Wisconsin in the early 1830s and 1840s to work in the lead mines that had been discovered there. One traditional dish that the miners ate often was the pasty (pronounced **pass**-tee). This is a handheld meat-and-vegetable pie that the Cornish workers brought with them into the mines so they could have a hearty lunch. Cornish children probably brought them to school, also. You can still find pasties on the menu at restaurants in towns like Mineral Point and Dodgeville. Pasties also are served at festivals and church suppers in the area. The Cornish sometimes served a homemade tomato sauce with pasties. Today you usually get ketchup, or sometimes salsa, with your pasty.

This recipe makes one very large pasty—too big for one person's lunch! Instead, you can divide this into four servings.

Directions:

1. Heat oven to 375 degrees. Line a baking sheet with parchment paper.

2. Place potatoes, carrots, onions, ground beef, butter bits, rosemary, thyme, salt, and pepper in a large bowl. Mix well. This mixture is the filling for the pasty.

3. Sprinkle about 2 tablespoons of flour over a clean table or countertop surface. Dust your hands with flour also. Remove the pie crust dough from its aluminum foil pan (if it is in one) and place it on the floured surface. Press the dough all around to flatten it out into a circle.

Ingredients:

1½ cups peeled and diced potatoes

½ cup peeled and diced carrots

¼ cup chopped onion

½ pound ground round beef

2 tablespoons cold or frozen butter, cut into small pieces

½ teaspoon dried rosemary

½ teaspoon dried thyme

1 teaspoon salt

¼ teaspoon black pepper

3–4 tablespoons flour to sprinkle over the table or countertop and to flour your hands

One 9-inch deep-dish pie crust, unbaked (and fully thawed, if it is frozen)

1 egg

You Will Need:

Baking sheet

Parchment paper

Sharp knife

Cutting board

Measuring cups and spoons

Large mixing bowl

Spatula (optional)

Small bowl

Fork

Pastry brush

4. Dump the filling in a mound in the center of the pie crust circle. Place your hands under half of the dough and fold it up and over the filling. Firmly press the top edge of the dough onto the bottom edge all around the filling. Fold the two edges together in small overlapping folds all along the pasty to seal it tightly.

5. Carefully transfer the pasty onto the prepared baking sheet. (You can do this with your hands, and use a spatula, too, if that makes it easier.) Beat the egg in a small bowl with a fork until smooth. Use a pastry brush to brush some of the beaten egg all over the pasty. (You can put the leftover egg in the refrigerator and use it for scrambled eggs the next morning.) Use a sharp knife to make 2 or 3 small slits in the top of the pasty (this will let the steam out as the pasty bakes).

6. Bake the pasty until it is golden brown all over, 45–55 minutes. Serve it hot (but don't burn your tongue!).

This woman in Linden, Wisconsin, was busy making Cornish pasties around 50 years ago. Her husband looks like he couldn't wait for a taste!

Rugelach

32 cookies

Cookies have been a sweet treat in Wisconsin since the first European immigrants settled here. The immigrants brought ethnic cookie recipes from their homelands. They served cookies for many kinds of occasions, such as barn raisings and threshings, but also during the holidays and when relatives came to visit. *Rugelach* are special cookies baked in many Jewish homes during Hanukkah, the Festival of Lights—and at other times of the year, too.

Directions:

1. Use a food processor or blender to blend cottage cheese until it is creamy and smooth.

Caution

This recipe calls for the use of a food processor, which has very sharp blades. Be sure an adult is present and watching closely when you are handling the food processor.

2. Place the creamed cottage cheese and butter in a large bowl. Beat with a wooden spoon until the ingredients are very well blended.

3. Stir in 2 cups flour to make a dough.

4. Divide the dough into 4 equal-sized balls. Wrap each dough ball in plastic wrap or waxed paper.

5. Place the balls in the refrigerator and let them chill until the dough is firm. This will take at least 2 hours.

Ingredients:

1 cup cottage cheese

1 cup (2 sticks) butter, softened

2 cups flour, plus extra for rolling out the dough

1 tablespoon ground cinnamon

⅓ cup sugar

½ cup raisins

½ cup chopped walnuts

You Will Need:

Measuring cups

Food processor or blender

Large bowl

Wooden spoon

Plastic wrap or waxed paper

Rolling pin

Knife

Cookie sheets

Wire cooling racks

6. Heat the oven to 400 degrees. While the oven is heating, sprinkle some flour on a clean table or countertop. Use a floured rolling pin to roll out one ball of dough on the flour. Roll it out into a circle that is about 8 to 9 inches wide. Do the same with the other 3 balls of dough.

7. Sprinkle each dough circle with one-quarter of the cinnamon, sugar, raisins, and walnuts.

8. Use a floured knife to cut each circle into 8 wedges (like a pie).

9. Roll up each wedge, starting from the wide end. Place the cookies at least 1 inch apart on ungreased cookie sheets.

10. Bake until the rugelach are lightly browned, 25–30 minutes.

11. Let them cool off on wire racks before serving them.

Sweet Potato Pie

8 servings

Holidays are often a time to celebrate our ethnic heritage through the foods we eat. Christmas and Hanukkah are two examples of this. Can you think of some special traditional foods that families eat during Christmas, Hanukkah, or other holidays?

Sweet potato pie is an African American dessert that is often served during Kwanzaa. Kwanzaa is an African American holiday that runs from December 26 to New Year's Day. On each day of Kwanzaa, families light a candle and discuss ideas about what's important in life. At the end of the week, they celebrate with a party where there is dancing, music, and, of course, delicious heritage foods.

Sweet potato pie is yummy, and this one at Milwaukee's African World Festival looks like it's ready to eat!

Directions:

1. Heat oven to 350 degrees. Line a baking sheet or pizza pan with parchment paper or aluminum foil.

2. In a large bowl combine the mashed sweet potatoes, melted butter, and sugar. Stir well.

3. Using a fork or wooden spoon, beat in the eggs 1 at a time.

How to Make Mashed Sweet Potatoes

Poke a couple of holes in each of the sweet potatoes with a fork. Place on the oven rack and bake at 350 degrees until the sweet potatoes are soft. This will take about 45–60 minutes. Let them cool for 10–15 minutes. Cut them open, scrape out the orange flesh into a large bowl, and then beat with an electric hand mixer or a fork until it is smooth.

Ingredients:

2½ cups mashed cooked sweet potatoes
(about 2 or 3 large sweet potatoes; see
mashing instructions on page 172)

4 tablespoons butter, melted

1 cup sugar

3 large eggs

1 cup half-and-half or heavy
whipping cream

1 teaspoon vanilla extract

1 teaspoon ground cinnamon

½ teaspoon salt

¼ teaspoon ground nutmeg

¼ teaspoon ground cloves

1 store-bought 9-inch pie crust
(in a foil pan), unbaked

You Will Need:

Measuring cups and spoons

Fork

Electric hand mixer (optional)

Baking sheet or pizza pan

Parchment paper or aluminum foil

Large bowl

Toothpicks

Wire cooling rack

Wooden spoon

4. Stir in the half-and-half (or heavy cream), vanilla, cinnamon, salt, nutmeg, and cloves.

5. Place the pie crust on the baking sheet or pizza pan. Pour the filling mixture into the pie crust.

6. Bake the pie until it no longer "jiggles" in the middle. This will take 45–55 minutes. You can check for doneness by poking a toothpick in the center of the pie. If it comes out clean, the pie is done.

7. Cool the pie to room temperature on a wire rack.

Southeast Asian Spring Rolls

About 12

Ingredients:

Spicy Dipping Sauce

1 cup water

¼ cup sugar

1 tablespoon fresh lime juice

1 tablespoon bottled fish sauce (available in large supermarkets and Asian grocery stores)

1 clove garlic, chopped and then mashed with a fork into small bits

1 or more Thai hot peppers or jalapeños, chopped and then mashed with a fork into small bits

Spring Rolls

4 ounces uncooked rice noodles or vermicelli (very thin spaghetti)

1 small head leaf lettuce

1 large cucumber

1 cup cilantro leaves

1 cup mint leaves

1 cup basil leaves

2 cups bean sprouts

1½ cups finely chopped cooked pork, chicken, or shrimp

1 package (12 ounces) 8-inch round spring roll skins (this is sometimes called "rice paper"; you can find it in large supermarkets and Asian grocery stores)

Spring rolls are a favorite food in Laos and Thailand, two countries from which Hmong families immigrated to Wisconsin after the Vietnam War. Spring rolls are fresh-tasting and fun to make. Try having a spring roll party: Put all the spring roll fillings in bowls and then have everyone make their own. That way, each person gets to put whatever he or she likes best into the rolls. Spring rolls are usually served as soon as they are assembled, but you can make them ahead of time and refrigerate them in an airtight container until you serve them.

These spring rolls are paired with a spicy sauce, but you can also serve them with peanut sauce, soy sauce, or other Asian sauces. And you can add other fillings if you like, such as green onions, radishes, and snow peas. (That's the fun of spring rolls—anything goes!)

Directions:

1. Prepare the Spicy Dipping Sauce: Combine water and sugar in a small saucepan. Bring to a boil and boil 2 minutes. Cool. Stir in lime juice, fish sauce, garlic, and hot peppers or jalapeños. Set aside.

2. To make the spring rolls: Bring a tea kettle of water to a boil, then turn down the heat to its lowest point so the water stays hot (but not simmering or boiling). Meanwhile, prepare the spring roll fillings as follows:

Caution!
Be sure to use plastic gloves when you are working with the hot peppers for the Spicy Dipping Sauce.

3. Cook the rice noodles or vermicelli according to the package instructions. Rinse them lightly and let them cool. Place the cooked, cooled noodles in a bowl.

4. Slice the lettuce into thin strips. Place them in a bowl.

5. Peel the cucumber. Cut it in half lengthwise. Scoop out the seeds with a spoon. Starting at one end, slice the cucumber halves very thinly. Place them in a bowl.

6. Place each kind of fresh herb in a bowl. Place the bean sprouts in a bowl. Place the pork, chicken, or shrimp in a bowl. Line up all the bowls on a table or work surface.

7. Now assemble the spring rolls: Pour some of the hot water from the tea kettle into a large, deep pan. For each spring roll: Dip 1 sheet of rice paper in the hot water. It will quickly become soft and "cooked." Carefully, so as not to burn your fingers, remove the softened rice paper and place it on a large plate. Soak another sheet and overlap it onto the first. Pile the following ingredients near the bottom of the overlapping rice paper: a few tablespoons of lettuce; 10–12 bean sprouts; 8–10 cucumber slivers; some noodles; 3–4 leaves of each herb; and 1–2 tablespoons of meat or shrimp. (Or layer whatever items and amounts you like!)

8. Roll up the spring roll: Fold the bottom edge up and over the filling. Fold the 2 side edges over the filling. Roll the spring roll from the bottom up, to seal the filling inside. (The softened rice paper will stick to itself where it overlaps.) Place the finished spring roll on a serving platter.

9. Continue to make spring rolls. You may need to add more hot water to the pan once in a while.

10. Serve the spring rolls with the dipping sauce.

You Will Need:

Measuring cups and spoons
Sharp knife
Cutting board
Fork and spoon
Plastic gloves
Small saucepan
Tea kettle of water
Pot in which to boil noodles
Bowls for the spring roll fillings
Vegetable peeler
Large, deep pan
Large plate
Large serving platter

Agua de Horchata (Mexican Cinnamon Milk)

16–20 servings

Agua de horchata (pronounced **ah**-gwah day or-**cha**-ta) is a tasty, cool drink that Mexican Americans brought to this country. You can often find it for sale at Mexican festivals such as Cinco de Mayo in Milwaukee.

Ingredients:

1 cup uncooked white rice

1 whole cinnamon stick, broken into 3 or 4 pieces

13 cups water

1 small can (14 ounces) sweetened condensed milk

1 cup milk

½ cup sugar

1 teaspoon vanilla extract

Ground cinnamon for sprinkling on each glassful

You Will Need:

Extra-large mixing bowl
Clean kitchen towel
1-gallon jug
Wooden spoon
Food processor or blender
Tall glasses
Ice cubes

Directions:

1. Combine the rice, broken-up cinnamon pieces, and water in an extra-large bowl. Cover it with a clean kitchen towel and let it stand at room temperature for 6–8 hours (or overnight). Soaking the rice like this will soften it.

2. Carefully, without disturbing the rice on the bottom, pour most of the water into a 1-gallon jug. Set the jug aside.

3. Remove the cinnamon pieces from the rice; set them aside. Add the condensed milk, milk, sugar, and vanilla extract to the rice. Stir it with a wooden spoon to mix well.

4. Working in batches, blend the rice mixture in a food processor or blender until it is as smooth as possible. This may take a minute or 2 for each batch. Pour each blended batch into the reserved water in the jug. When all the batches are done, stir the cinnamon pieces into the mixture in the jug. Cover and chill for 2 hours or longer, until you're ready to serve it.

5. To serve: Fill tall glasses with ice cubes. Stir the mixture well and pour it over the ice. Garnish each glassful with a sprinkling of ground cinnamon.

Caution

This recipe calls for the use of a food processor, which has very sharp blades. Be sure an adult is present and watching closely when you are handling the food processor.

Blueberry Yogurt Parfaits

4–6 servings

Wisconsin is a region of many kinds of food—and many kinds of food celebrations! We celebrate everything from cheese, brats, and corn to trout, watermelon, and chocolate. There is even a festival that honors blueberries. It takes place every July in the little town of Iron River, in Bayfield County in the far northern part of the state, where blueberries grow well.

Directions:

1. Place 2–3 tablespoons of granola in the bottom of each cup.

2. Add 2–3 tablespoons of yogurt to each cup, and then 2–3 tablespoons of blueberries.

3. Keep making layers of the granola, yogurt, and berries until they are all used up.

Ingredients:

2 cups granola

1½ cups vanilla yogurt

1–2 cups blueberries

You Will Need:

4–6 clear-glass dessert cups or glasses

Spoons

Blueberries are packed with vitamin A—and blueberry goodness!

Hull Corn Soup

8 or more servings

Hull corn is a type of white corn that has been hulled—meaning the outer covering of the corn kernel has been removed. It is the basis for a traditional Native American soup. Some tribes enjoy hull corn soup at powwows, which are Indian celebrations of culture, family, and friendship. Oneida Indians in northeastern Wisconsin raise white corn and process it into hull corn. They also make and can hull corn soup and offer it for sale from a tribal store.

Many Mexican families make a similar soup called *posole* (pronounced poh-**zoh**-lay). The English word for the hulled corn in posole is *hominy* (pronounced **hom**-in-nee). Mexicans add hot peppers and fresh garnishes such as shredded cabbage, chopped cilantro, sliced radishes, and lime juice to posole.

This recipe is similar to the Indian version of hull corn soup. But if you want to make the Mexican version, add 1 tablespoon chopped garlic, 2 teaspoons dried oregano, and 1 teaspoon cumin to the soup along with the other ingredients. Then serve it with the garnishes described above.

You can find canned hull corn, or hominy, at Latino food markets or in the Mexican foods section in most large grocery stores.

Ingredients:

1 can (29 ounces) hominy or white corn, rinsed and drained

1 pound lean ground pork

10 cups chicken stock or water (or you may use a combination of both)

1 cup chopped onion

1 can (15 ounces) kidney or pinto beans, rinsed and drained

Salt and black pepper

You Will Need:

Sharp knife
Cutting board
Colander
Soup pot with lid
Measuring cup
Large spoon

Directions:

1. Place hominy, pork, stock or water, and onion in a soup pot. Stir the mixture, then bring it to a simmer, uncovered. As it is heating up, use a large spoon to skim off any scum that rises to the top. You may need to do this several times.

2. Add the beans. Cover the soup and let it simmer over very low heat for about 1 hour. Add water if you need more liquid to keep it soupy.

3. Season to taste with salt and pepper.

Strawberry Mini Cheesecake Cups

4 servings

If you attend a Wisconsin farm breakfast, be sure to bring your appetite!

Since Wisconsin is the Dairy State, it's no surprise that many kinds of dairy events take place here. There's the Great Wisconsin Cheese Festival in Little Chute, Cheese Days in Monroe, and Cows on the Concourse in Madison. Each June many Wisconsin counties also host an on-the-farm dairy breakfast, complete with such dairy treats as scrambled eggs with cheese, French toast, and milk shakes (yes, milk shakes for breakfast!). Here is a recipe to serve at your own "dairy party."

Directions:

1. Place a tea kettle of water over high heat and bring it to a boil. Heat oven to 325 degrees. Place 4 six-ounce custard cups in a square baking pan.

2. While the water and oven are heating, make the filling: Place the cream cheese, heavy cream, eggs, grated orange peel, and vanilla extract in a mixing bowl. Use an electric mixer to whip the mixture until smooth, stopping 2 or 3 times to scrape down the sides of the bowl with a rubber spatula.

Ingredients:

1 package (8 ounces) cream
   cheese, brought to room
   temperature

½ cup heavy cream

2 eggs

2 teaspoons finely grated
   orange peel (grate only the
   outer, orange-colored part
   of the orange)

¾ teaspoon vanilla extract

1½ cups fresh strawberries

2 tablespoons honey

You Will Need:

Grater

Tea kettle of water

4 six-ounce custard cups

Square baking pan

2 medium mixing bowls

Measuring cups and spoons

Electric mixer

Rubber spatula

Aluminum foil

Wire cooling rack

Spoon

Plastic wrap

Sharp knife

Cutting board

3. Spoon the batter into the cups. Slowly add boiling water to the pan (don't forget
to use hot pads!), enough to come halfway up the sides of the cups. Cover the
pan with aluminum foil. Bake 30 minutes.

4. Turn the oven off and let the pan with the cups stand in the oven 20 minutes.
Remove from the oven, uncover, and cool completely on a wire cooling rack.
Cover the cups with plastic wrap. Put them in the refrigerator to chill for 1 hour
or longer.

5. A few minutes before you're ready to serve the cheesecakes, slice the
strawberries. Place them in a bowl and toss them gently with the honey. Divide
the berries evenly among the cups, placing them on top of the cheesecakes.

Acknowledgments

We thank the following individuals and organizations for generously allowing us to use their photographs in *The Flavor of Wisconsin for Kids:* John Baker; Jeanne Carpenter of Wisconsin Cheese Originals; Gerry Emmerich; Connie Ghiloni; Hollands family farm; Bill Lubing; the Voight family; Zane Williams; Bayfield Chamber of Commerce and Visitor Bureau; *Capital Times;* Community Action Coalition for South Central Wisconsin, Inc.; Driftless Organics; *Edible Madison/ Edible Communities, Inc.;* Great Lakes Fish & Wildlife Commission; Growing Power; Harmony Valley Farm; Hoard Historical Museum; Organic Valley; Royal Ontario Museum; University of Wisconsin–Madison College of Agriculture and Life Sciences/*Grow magazine;* USDA/NASS Milk Production; Wisconsin Cartographers' Guild; Wisconsin Department of Natural Resources; Wisconsin Department of Tourism; Wisconsin State Cranberry Growers Association.

For testing several recipes, thanks to Maddie Holman; Jill, Ruth, and Alynn McLeod; Mia Thompson; and Althea Wincek.

Our greatest gratitude and admiration go to editors Kate Thompson and Barbara Walsh, those masters of book improvement. We couldn't have done it without you.

Thank you to Terese's husband, Jim Block, the one she can never thank enough, and to Bobbie's spouse, Bill Malone, lifetime love and partner. And, from Terese, a happy nod to Washington Island, which she thinks is the best place on the planet to write, while Bobbie prefers her laptop out on the back porch when the weather cooperates.

Finally, a high five and a thousand thanks to each other: Bobbie, the "kid-ifier," and Terese, the "food-ifier." To our readers, we say, "Happy cooking, eating, and learning!"

About the Authors

Terese Allen has written many books and articles about Wisconsin's food traditions and culinary culture, including *The Flavor of Wisconsin*, the 2012 *Wisconsin Local Foods Journal*, and *Cafe Wisconsin Cookbook*. She is food editor for Organic Valley and a columnist for *Edible Madison* magazine. Terese serves as president of the Culinary History Enthusiasts of Wisconsin (CHEW) and is the former chair of the REAP Food Group, a food and sustainability organization in southern Wisconsin.

As director of the Office of School Services at the Wisconsin Historical Society, **Bobbie Malone** wrote, co-wrote, and edited many books for classrooms,

including the fourth-grade textbook, *Wisconsin: Our State, Our Story*, the New Badger History series, and the Badger Biographies series. Now she consults with school districts and museums and is busily working on a biography of author-illustrator Lois Lenski.

Illustration Credits

Photographs identified with WHi are from the Society's collections; address requests to reproduce these photos to the Visual Materials Archivist at the Wisconsin Historical Society, 816 State Street, Madison, WI 53706. Credits read clockwise from the upper left of each page.

Frontmatter **Page 1** Title image, illustration by Michael Custode. **Page 3** Boy drinking in wheat field, WHi Image ID 46940. **Page 4** Fall birch trees, courtesy of the Wisconsin Department of Tourism; Nuts and leaves, illustration by Michael Custode; Fish, illustration by Michael Custode; Fishing at night, photo by RJ and Linda Miller, courtesy of the Wisconsin Department of Tourism; Pea pod, illustration by Michael Custode; Farm with cornfield, courtesy of Organic Valley, organicvalley. coop. **Page 5** Farm with cows, photo by Donald S. Abrams, courtesy of the Wisconsin Department of Tourism; Cheese wheel, illustration by Michael Custode; Garden, photo by Gerald H. Emmerich Jr.; Squash, illustration by Michael Custode; Hmong girls, photo by Gene Staver, courtesy of the Wisconsin Department of Tourism; Rolling pin and dough, illustration by Michael Custode. **Page 6** Little girls having a tea party, WHi Image ID 83832; Kids baking, WHi Image ID 34423. **Page 7** Sculpting cheese, courtesy of the Wisconsin Department of Tourism; Kids making butter, WHi Image ID 68601. **Page 8** Girl with box of apples, courtesy of the Wisconsin Department of Tourism. **Page 9** Kids milking cow, photo by Gene Staver, courtesy of the Wisconsin Department of Tourism; Fishing in Washington County, photo by Donald S. Abrams, courtesy of the Wisconsin Department of Tourism; Kids eating ice cream, WHi Image ID 56988.

Chapter 1 **Page 11** Fall birch trees, courtesy of the Wisconsin Department of Tourism; Nuts and leaves, illustration by Michael Custode. **Page 12** Early Wisconsin spear points: (top) courtesy of the University of Wisconsin Geology Museum, (middle) WHS Museum # 1951.1128, (bottom) courtesy of the

Wisconsin Historical Society Archaeology Program; Archaic Indian deer hunters, WHi Image ID 33814. **Page 13** Hunters with rabbits, WHi Image ID 58408; Hunters at their cabin, WHi Image ID 24434; Boy hunter with his deer, courtesy of the Wisconsin Department of Natural Resources. **Page 14** Ripe raspberries, courtesy of the Bayfield Chamber of Commerce and Visitor Bureau; Ramps, photo by Bill Lubing; Blueberry pickers, WHi Image ID 78031. **Page 15** Morel mushroom, courtesy of the Wisconsin Department of Tourism. **Page 16** Indian sugar camp, WHi Image ID 5224; Maple leaf, © iStockphoto/ Samantha Grandy. **Page 17** Maple leaf, © iStockphoto/ Samantha Grandy; Indian mocock, WHS Museum # 1963.194.25. **Page 18** Elizabeth Fisher, WHi Image ID 5210; Girl tasting sap, photo by Donald S. Abrams, courtesy of the Wisconsin Department of Tourism. **Page 19** Lumberjacks eating, WHi Image ID 5777. **Page 20** Deer hunters, WHi Image ID 28304. **Page 22** Deer standing in grasses, photo by Molly Rose Teuke, courtesy of the Wisconsin Department of Tourism. **Page 28** Girls gathering raspberries, WHi Image ID 47361. **Page 29** Blueberries, © iStockphoto/ Vitalina Rybakova. **Page 30** Hickory nuts, photo by Bill Lubing. **Page 32** Maple syrup, photo by Bill Lubing. **Page 35** Pastry blender and biscuit cutter, illustrations by Audrey Durney.

Chapter 2 **Page 36** Map by Earth Illustrated, Inc. **Page 37** Fish, illustration by Michael Custode; Fishing at night, photo by RJ and Linda Miller, courtesy of the Wisconsin Department of Tourism. **Page 38** Fisherman with equipment, WHi Image ID 2061; Fishing on breakwater, WHi Image ID 6941. **Page 39** Menominee spearfishing by torchlight, courtesy of the Royal Ontario Museum; Ice harvesting, WHi Image ID 11341. **Page 40** Commercial fishermen, WHi Image ID 78115; Muskie caught at Ross's Teal Lake Lodge, WHi Image ID 37955. **Page 41** Color image of fish boil, photo by Jim Klousia for Edible Madison; Black-and-white image of fish boil, WHi Image ID 63378. **Page 42** Beavers, WHi Image ID 35065; Duck hunters, WHi Image ID 74092. **Page 43** Indian women harvesting wild rice, WHi Image ID 9023; Wild rice beds, courtesy of Great Lakes Indian Fish & Wildlife Commission.

Page 44 Ojibwe man harvesting wild rice, courtesy of the Wisconsin Department of Tourism. **Page 45** Cranberries, courtesy of the Wisconsin State Cranberry Growers Association; Ho-Chunk harvesting cranberries, WHi Image ID 24507. **Page 46** Harvesting cranberries, courtesy of the Wisconsin State Cranberry Growers Association. **Page 47** Hands holding cranberries, courtesy of the Wisconsin State Cranberry Growers Association; Glass of cranberry juice, © iStockphoto/Merlin Farwell. **Page 48** Fishermen with catch, WHi Image ID 49874. **Page 49** Lemon juicer, illustration by Audrey Durney; Fishing on dock, photo by Brian Malloy, courtesy of the Wisconsin Department of Tourism. **Page 52** Duck in water, © iStockphoto/ Dennys Bisogno. **Page 57** Sorting cranberries, courtesy of the Wisconsin State Cranberry Growers Association. **Page 59** Grater and lemon juicer, illustrations by Audrey Durney.

Chapter 3 **Page 61** Farm with cornfield, courtesy of Organic Valley, organicvalley.coop; Pea pod, illustration by Michael Custode. **Page 62** Drawing of shovel plow, WHi Image ID 55377; Farmers harvesting wheat, WHi Image ID 26280. **Page 63** Men with plow, WHi Image ID 1984; McCormick catalog cover, WHi Image ID 4281. **Page 64** Harvesting potatoes, WHi Image ID 58415. **Page 65** Hops, WHi Image ID 30472. **Page 66** Tall-tale postcard, WHi Image ID 44424; Vegetables at Union High School, WHi Image ID 66430. **Page 67** Inspecting peas, WHi Image ID 42532; Klindt-Geiger pickles, WHi Image ID 81106. **Page 68** Golden Delicious apples, photo by RJ and Linda Miller, courtesy of the Wisconsin Department of Tourism. **Page 69** Picking cherries, WHi Image ID 77918; Door County cherry blossoms, photo by Donald S. Abrams, courtesy of the Wisconsin Department of Tourism. **Page 70** Hmong vendor at farmers' market, photo by Bill Lubing. **Page 71** CSA box, photo by Mike Lind for Driftless Organics Farm. **Page 72** Will Allen, courtesy of Growing Power. **Page 73** Summer vegetables, photo by Bill Lubing. **Page 74** Harvested wheat, WHi Image ID 46952. **Page 76** Red, white, and blue potatoes, photo by Bill Lubing. **Page 77** Grater, illustration by Audrey Durney. **Page 80** Governor Phil La Follette with peas, WHi Image ID 45229. **Page 82** Man with big cabbage, WHi Image ID 1982. **Page 84** Honey, photo by Bill Lubing. **Page 86** Apples, photo by Don Albrecht, courtesy of the Wisconsin Department of Tourism. **Page 88** Students making applesauce, WHi Image ID 61681. **Page 90** Orchard sign, photo by Gary Knowles, courtesy of the Wisconsin Department of Tourism. **Page 91** Picking raspberries, photo by Mary Langenfeld, courtesy of the Wisconsin Department of Tourism. **Page 92** Cucumbers, © iStockphoto/Viktor Lugovskoy. **Page 93** Tomatoes, © iStockphoto/tomch; Asparagus, © iStockphoto/RedHelga.

Chapter 4 **Page 95** Cheese wheel, illustration by Michael Custode; Farm with cows, photo by Donald S. Abrams, courtesy of the Wisconsin Department of Tourism. **Page 96** Woman with cow, WHi Image ID 2016; Chatty Belle statue, photo by RJ and Linda Miller, courtesy of the Wisconsin Department of Tourism. **Page 97** Silo under construction, WHi Image ID 37268; Kids feeding cows, WHi Image ID 23928. **Page 98** Stephen Babcock, WHi Image ID 5585; Phyllis Paulson, WHi Image ID 33802. **Page 99** Hoard's Dairyman cover, courtesy of Hoard's Dairyman. **Page 100** Casper Jaggi, WHi Image ID 33258. **Page 101** Dairy promotion poster, WHi Image ID 42397; Edelweiss Creamery Swiss cheese wheel, photo by Shane Van Boxtel, courtesy of the Wisconsin Department of Tourism. **Page 102** Dairy farms production chart, USDA/NASS Milk Production, illustration by Jill Bremigan; Cows at Hemstead farm, courtesy of Organic Valley, organicvalley.coop. **Page 103** Artisan cheeses, Wolfgang Hoffmann/UW–Madison College of Agricultural and Life Sciences; Cheesemaker Marieke Penterman, courtesy of Hollands Family Farm. **Page 104** Brats at Taste of Madison, photo by Donald S. Abrams, courtesy of the Wisconsin Department of Tourism; Palmyra meat market, WHi Image ID 9351. **Page 105** Racing sausages, courtesy of Milwaukee Brewers Baseball Club; Women making sausages, WHi Image ID 37403. **Page 106** Churning butter by hand, WHi Image ID 85738. **Page 108** Cream puffs, WHi Image ID 26192. **Page 113** Knife, illustration by Audrey Durney. **Page 114** Sausages in window, Milwaukee Journal photo by Niels Lauritzen; WHi Image ID 85570. **Page 117** Girl stirring pot, WHi

Image ID 43904. **Page 120** Members of the Pleasant Ridge community, WHi Image ID 45972.

Chapter 5 **Page 123** Squash, illustration by Michael Custode; Garden, photo by Gerald H. Emmerich Jr. **Page 124** Ho-Chunk woman shucking corn, WHi Image ID 45751. **Page 125** Corn on the cob, © iStockphoto/Stefanie Timmermann; Belle La Follette working in the garden, WHi Image ID 29988. **Page 126** Fourteen-foot tomato plant, WHi Image ID 15357; Kohler family garden, WHi Image ID 1791. **Page 127** Schulz Garden at Old World Wisconsin, photo by Gerald H. Emmerich Jr. **Page 128** Sweet potatoes, photo courtesy of Bill Lubing; Root cellar, WHi Image ID 82767. **Page 129** Woman canning peppers, WHi Image ID 8321; Home canning advertisement, WHi Image ID 66866. **Page 130** International Harvester advertisement, WHi Image ID 4762; Boy at Community Chest Garden, WHi Image ID 59713. **Page 131** Girl watering garden, photo by Taylor Barrett, courtesy of the Community Action Coalition for South Central Wisconsin, Inc. **Page 132** Garden worms, photo by Chris Brockel, courtesy of the Community Action Coalition for South Central Wisconsin, Inc.; Garden shovel, © iStockphoto/Nick M. Do. **Page 133** Rooftop garden, © Zane Williams; Backyard chicken, photo by John Baker—backyardchickens.com. **Page 134** Modern spider, photo by Ellen S. Penwell, Old World Wisconsin. **Page 136** Boy eating corn, photo by Mary Langenfeld, courtesy of the Wisconsin Department of Tourism. **Page 138** Winter squash, photo by Bill Lubing. **Page 140** Boy sitting on pumpkin, WHi Image ID 86034. **Page 144** Red and yellow tomatoes, photo by Bill Lubing. **Page 146** Harvesting cucumbers, WHi Image ID 38714. **Page 147** Mint plant, © 2012 by Carole Topalian for Edible Communities, Inc. **Page 148** Strawberries, photo by Donald S. Abrams, courtesy of the Wisconsin Department of Tourism. **Page 150** Woman with egg basket, WHi Image ID 75320. **Page 151** Handheld eggbeater, illustration by Audrey Durney.

Chapter 6 **Page 153** Hmong girls, photo by Gene Staver, courtesy of the Wisconsin Department of

Tourism; Rolling pin and dough, illustration by Michael Custode. **Page 154** Goldenberger family wurst roast, WHi Image ID 1971; William Tell Fest, photo by RJ and Linda Miller, courtesy of the Wisconsin Department of Tourism. **Page 155** European settlement, map by Wisconsin Cartographers' Guild, from Mapping Wisconsin History. **Page 156** Pleasant Ridge schoolhouse, WHi Image ID 4239; Howard's Bakery kringle, photo by Donald S. Abrams, courtesy of the Wisconsin Department of Tourism. **Page 157** Migrant cherry pickers, WHi Image ID 48938. **Page 158** Seder dinner, WHi Image ID 13055. **Page 159** Fried fish, Mike Devries/The Capital Times. **Page 160** Norwegian church supper, WHi Image ID 2100; Festa Italiana, photo by Donald S. Abrams, courtesy of the Wisconsin Department of Tourism. **Page 161** Oktoberfest, photo by RJ and Linda Miller, courtesy of the Wisconsin Department of Tourism; Ho-Chunk woman preparing fry bread, WHi Image ID 65806. **Page 162** Kraut Festival, photo by Donald S. Abrams, courtesy of the Wisconsin Department of Tourism; Two boys eating ice cream, photo by Donald S. Abrams, courtesy of the Wisconsin Department of Tourism. **Page 163** Farm family having dinner, WHi Image ID 85764; Norwegian women making sandbakkels, WHi Image ID 58397. **Page 164** Syttende Mai celebration, photo by Andy Kraushaar, courtesy of the Wisconsin Department of Tourism. **Page 167** Pastry brush, illustration by Audrey Durney. **Page 168** Cornish miners, WHi Image ID 8991. **Page 169** Woman making pasties, WHi Image ID 58386. **Page 169** Pastry brush, illustration by Audrey Durney. **Page 172** Sweet potato pie, photo by Donald S. Abrams, courtesy of the Wisconsin Department of Tourism. **Page 177** Blueberries, photo by Terese Allen. **Page 178** Hull corn, © iStockphoto/Yaiza Fernandez Garcia. **Page 180** Farm breakfast, photo by Gene Staver, courtesy of the Wisconsin Department of Tourism.

Backmatter **Page 182** Family eating watermelon, WHi Image ID 85523. **Page 183** Terese Allen, photo by Joel Heiman; Bobbie Malone, photo by Joel Heiman.

General Index

Note: Page numbers in *italics* refer to illustrations.

Recipe Index

A

African American dishes
  Black-Eyed Peas with Ham Hocks, 120–121
  Sweet Potato Pie, 172–173
Agua de Horchata (Mexican Cinnamon Milk), 176
American Indian dishes
  Baked Whitefish, 48–49
  Hull Corn Soup, 178–179
  Smoked Fish Cream Cheese Spread, 51
  Spider Johnnycake, 134–135
  Wild Rice with Egg Strips, 54–55
appetizers. *See* snacks
apples
  Apple Butter, 86–87
  Apple Kuchen, 88–89

B

Baked Whitefish, 48–49
Barley with Mushrooms, 26
beans
  Black-Eyed Peas with Ham Hocks, 120–121
beef
  Easy Cornish Pasties, 168–169
  Italian-Style Venison Meatloaf, 20–21
  Larb, 118–119
  Norwegian Meatballs, 164–165
  Venison Chili, 22–23
berries
  Blueberry Yogurt Parfaits, 177
  Chocolate-Dipped Strawberries, 148–149
  Cranberry Raspberry Smoothie, 57
  Mulled Cranberry Orange Drink, 59

Strawberry Mini Cheesecake Cups, 180–181
  Wild Berries and Honey, 28–29
beverages. *See* drinks
biscuits: Cookee's Biscuits, 34–35
Black-Eyed Peas with Ham Hocks, 120–121
blueberries: Blueberry Yogurt Parfaits, 177
brats: Bratwurst Vegetable Soup, 116–117
breads
  Cookee's Biscuits, 34–35
  Irish American Soda Bread, 74–75
  Spider Johnnycake, 134–135
  Worstenbroodjes (Dutch "Pigs in a Blanket"), 166–167
breakfast dishes
  Apple Kuchen, 88–89
  Blueberry Yogurt Parfaits, 177
  Cookee's Biscuits, 34–35
  Cranberry Raspberry Smoothie, 57
  Creamy Scrambled Eggs with Ramps or Green Onions, 27
  Homemade Butter, 106–107
  Maple Butter Spread, 33
  Potato Pancakes, 76–77
  Sausage Potato Cakes, 114–115
  Schmorn, 150–151
  Wild Berries and Honey, 28–29
  Wild Rice Pudding with Dried Cherries, 55
  Wild Rice with Egg Strips, 54
butter
  Butter-Glazed Carrot Coins with Fresh Mint, 147
  Homemade Butter, 106–107
  Maple Butter Spread, 33

C

cabbage: Soda Bottle Sauerkraut, 82–83
cakes
  Holiday Hickory Nut (or Butternut) Cake, 30–31

"Pick Your Own" Fruit Custard Cake, 90–91
  Spider Johnnycake, 134–135
carrots: Butter-Glazed Carrot Coins with Fresh Mint, 147
cheese
  Cheesy Smashed Potatoes with Toasted Nuts, 78–79
  CSA Veggies and Dip, 92–93
  Easy Tomato Feta Sauce (for Pasta, Rice, or Couscous), 113
  Honey Nut Cottage Cheese Pie, 84–85
  Quesadillas, 112
  Smoked Fish Cream Cheese Spread, 51
  Strawberry Mini Cheesecake Cups, 180–181
  Wisconsin Cheese and Sausage Platter, 111
cherries
  Duck with Door County Cherries, 52–53
  Wild Rice Pudding with Dried Cherries, 55
chicken: Rabbit (or Chicken) with Mushroom Sauce, 24–25
chili: Venison Chili, 22–23
Chocolate-Dipped Strawberries, 148–149
Chunky Pickled Garden Cukes, 146
Cookee's Biscuits, 34–35
cookies
  Cranberry Pecan Cookies, 58
  Pumpkin Cookies, 140–141
  Rugelach, 170–171
corn
  Corn on the Cob, 136–137
  Fresh Corn and Tomato Salsa, 142–143
  Hull Corn Soup, 178–179
Cornish dishes: Easy Cornish Pasties, 168–169
cornmeal: Spider Johnnycake, 134–135
cranberries
  Cranberry Pecan Cookies, 58
  Cranberry Raspberry Smoothie, 57
  Fresh Cranberry Relish, 56
  Mulled Cranberry Orange Drink, 59

cream
  Cream Puffs, 108–109
  Real Whipped Cream, 110
Creamy Scrambled Eggs with Ramps or Green Onions, 27
cucumbers: Chunky Pickled Garden Cukes, 146–147

D

desserts
  Apple Kuchen, 88–89
  Blueberry Yogurt Parfaits, 177
  Chocolate-Dipped Strawberries, 148–149
  Cranberry Pecan Cookies, 58
  Cranberry Raspberry Smoothie, 57
  Cream Puffs, 108–109
  Holiday Hickory Nut (or Butternut) Cake, 30–31
  Honey Nut Cottage Cheese Pie, 84–85
  Maple Cream Sundaes, 32
  "Pick Your Own" Fruit Custard Cake, 90–91
  Pumpkin Cookies, 140–141
  Real Whipped Cream, 110
  Rugelach, 170–171
  Strawberry Mini Cheesecake Cups, 180–181
  Sweet Potato Pie, 172–173
  Wild Berries and Honey, 28–29
  Wild Rice Pudding with Dried Cherries, 55
dips
  CSA Veggies and Dip, 92–93
  Fresh Corn and Tomato Salsa, 142–143
drinks
  Agua de Horchata (Mexican Cinnamon Milk), 176
  Cranberry Raspberry Smoothie, 57
  Mulled Cranberry Orange Drink, 59
Duck with Door County Cherries, 52–53
Dutch dishes: Worstenbroodjes (Dutch "Pigs in a Blanket"), 166–167